LEAVING
BUDDHA

LEAVING BUDDHA

*A Tibetan Monk's Encounter
with the Living God*

TENZIN LAHKPA
with EUGENE BACH

WHITAKER
HOUSE

LEAVING BUDDHA:
A Tibetan Monk's Encounter with the Living God

Eugene Bach
BacktoJerusalem.com

ISBN: 978-1-64123-102-2
eBook ISBN: 978-1-64123-103-9
Printed in the United States of America
© 2019 by Back to Jerusalem, Inc.

Whitaker House
1030 Hunt Valley Circle
New Kensington, PA 15068
www.whitakerhouse.com

Library of Congress Cataloging-in-Publication Data
Names: Lahkpa, Tenzin, 1969- author. | Bach, Eugene, author.
Title: Leaving Buddha : a Tibetan Monk's encounter with the living God /
  Tenzin Lahkpa with Eugene Bach.
Description: New Kensington, PA : Whitaker House, [2019] | Includes
  bibliographical references. |
Identifiers: LCCN 2019001398 (print) | LCCN 2019005065 (ebook) | ISBN
  9781641231039 (ebook) | ISBN 9781641231022 (trade pbk. : alk. paper)
Subjects: LCSH: Lahkpa, Tenzin, 1969- | Christian converts from Buddhism.
Classification: LCC BV2618.4.L34 (ebook) | LCC BV2618.4.L34 A3 2019 (print) |
  DDC 248.2/4643—dc23
LC record available at https://lccn.loc.gov/2019001398

2 3 4 5 6 7 8 9 10 11 12 **W** 26 25 24 23 22 21 20 19

Contents

Part Three: Enlightened by Love and Sacrifice

A Note from the Coauthor

When I began to write this book, my relationship with Tenzin Lahkpa (a pseudonym) was completely new. I met him at a lunch meeting in August 2017 in western China, where our Back to Jerusalem missionary team was discussing a project to reach out to the Tibetan people. One of the pastors brought along Tenzin, a former Buddhist monk, who shared his personal testimony at the table.

When I heard Tenzin's story, I was speechless. I was so moved and inspired by his experiences that I knew right away this was a story that needed to be shared with others.

Tenzin is not the first Buddhist monk I have met who has come to Christ (although I believe the number is relatively few), but he is the first to allow me to share his amazing story. Every time I sat down at my computer to write his personal account, I trembled with fear, knowing that it was a special project—one I did not feel qualified for due to the challenges and intricacies involved.

The first challenge was to obtain a full version of his story. I had asked Tenzin to write down his experiences so that I could translate them and make his life story available to others—but what I received was a very humble, two-page biography! Additional information came during subsequent interviews where Tenzin felt embarrassed and extremely reluctant to talk about himself. As a Buddhist monk, he had been instructed for years to remove any sign of self-identity in an effort to obtain enlightenment. Talking about his own story and focusing on himself was the exact opposite of what he had been taught to do. Furthermore, like many Christians living in Tibet today, Tenzin does not see himself as anything special. He is simple and unassuming. If you were to meet him on the street, you would most likely not think twice about him.

The second challenge was that I was convinced my level of facility in the Chinese and Tibetan languages was not high enough to adequately translate Tenzin's experiences. Thus, this book was written from a series of interviews conducted in 2017 and 2018 by five of my close colleagues and translated from Amdo Tibetan to Mandarin Chinese and eventually to English.

Third, in October 2017, a political development greatly hindered the interview process and the challenge of verifying an accurate translation of Tenzin's story. The Chinese Communist Party came together in Beijing and passed new oppressive religious laws that came into effect on February 1, 2018. Thus, the interviews with Tenzin were carried out illegally and in secret during some of the most intense crackdowns on Christianity in China in more than a decade.

Fourth, even after scouring the material and running it by Tenzin and the translators, I still felt certain there were things I had missed or did not understand that were important. I also thought there are things I might have misunderstood or translated incorrectly. However, I have checked and double-checked the facts and events in this story to the best of my ability.

Even with these limitations and difficulties, I still believed sharing the story of Tenzin's life and his search for enlightenment was worth the tremendous hurdles needed to communicate it. His experiences give us a greater understanding of those who live in a closed and persecuted part of the world, of the branches and beliefs of Buddhism, of the universal search for truth, and of the God who is always ready to reach out to those who seek Him.

And so, in addition to the process described above, I used the following methodology to bring Tenzin's story to Western readers. I drew on my personal experiences and resources from working and traveling in Tibet for almost twenty years, which helped me to express some parts of the story in a deeper way than I could if I had only included the specific words Tenzin spoke during our interviews. I also added descriptions as a way to familiarize my audience with the unfamiliar. Even though Tenzin has journeyed to Nepal and India, he has never traveled to a non-Buddhist area of the world. He is only familiar with Tibetan Buddhist culture, aside for brief periods of contact with Western visitors like myself. Consequently, he is unable to identify with a reader who might not know what a typical Tibetan setting, practice, or ceremony might look like and therefore would be unable to offer a comparison or explanation to help them understand it. Additionally, I have described people, places, smells, practices, and ceremonies using auxiliary information.

For security reasons, many names, places, and events have been changed to protect Tenzin's identity. In order to bring clarity to certain aspects of the story, several conversations, people, places, and experiences were added that did not actually happen or did not exist. Some details, names, places, and people have also been added to the story to replace real events that might be a security risk to people if they were to be shared. Also, certain foreign missionaries and charity organizations have been involved in Tenzin's life and have played a significant part in his testimony, but they have been purposefully omitted from his story in order to protect the secrecy of their ongoing work and their presence in China and Tibet.

I acknowledge that the methodology used to convey Tenzin's story is both a strength and a weakness of this book—it takes its readers into the sights, sounds, color, and outlook of Tenzin's world to help them understand it, but ultimately these features can only be representative of many of his experiences. They allow for a story that is strongly based on Tenzin's life but, for the above reasons, necessarily includes aspects he did not personally express or experience.

Therefore, with full disclosure, by adding these descriptions and explanations, I have attempted to explain Tenzin's story in the clearest and fullest way possible. Even as I have done all this, I have humbly tried to write Tenzin's story as close to his direct words as possible and to present his story as a first-person account.

—*Eugene Bach*

Acknowledgments

I am humbled to think that I have been given the opportunity to attempt to share the special story of Brother Tenzin Lahkpa and his amazing journey to Christ. This journey would not be have been possible without the sacrifice of a great many people. For security reasons, I am not even able to mention many of those who were involved in the writing of this story.

I would especially like to thank the Tibetan translator. She translated for Tenzin for this book following the death of her husband. While suffering from loss and grief, she still found the strength to do this work because she strongly believed his story needed to get out to the world.

Without a doubt, two of the greatest blessings during this time were Belinda Chadwell and Ruth Chang (not her real name). They left their families during very busy times, traveled across the globe into the most remote areas of Tibet, and captured many portions of this story in order to fill in missing parts. They wove through the almost impossible maze of translating from Tibetan to Mandarin Chinese to English, and then back to Mandarin, and back to Tibetan—only to do it all over again, hour after hour and day after day. Without them, this story might never have been told to a wide audience.

Each time I met with Tenzin, his mentor—a Chinese pastor and good friend—was right there beside him. This mentor will never know how much of a help he was in enabling us to understand some of the more difficult details of the culture.

A huge dose of gratitude goes to the Back to Jerusalem manager from the Beijing office. For security reasons, I will not even attempt to give him a pseudonym, but he arranged each meeting with Tenzin during 2017 and 2018—the most intense years for persecution against the Christian church in China in recent years. At a time when many pastors and leaders were going underground and cutting off all contact with foreigners, the BTJ manager took the risk in order to tell this story.

I would also like to thank my good friends at AVC International in Switzerland. For two wonderful decades, I have had the privilege to serve together with them as they have tirelessly supported so many workers and evangelists in China like Tenzin.

Of course, this book would never even have gotten into print if it were not for Bob Whitaker and his sweet daughter Christine. They and their team at Whitaker House are more than ministry partners. They are close friends that Christ has brought into my life to bring amazing testimonies into the library of Christian history.

Of all the people whom I have to acknowledge, few are more precious than Joyce Meyer and her son David, who have given untold resources for ministry to Tibet. Without fanfare, they have pushed toward the goal of getting the gospel into the hands of the Tibetan people. It was during an operation that was supported by their ministry that I first met with Tenzin and heard his testimony of leaving Buddha and becoming a follower of Christ.

Prologue: The Great Debate

I was running at the back of the crowd, trying to peek over the shoulders of the village elders who were sitting at the front of the gathering. I kept jumping in the air, looking for the perfect view, but as soon as I was able to find a gap between shoulders or arms, someone would sway and block my view again.

I wanted to witness the debate in our village between two of the most well-known and respected Tibetan *lamas* in our area. I do not remember their names, but I remember the event. I was very young at the time and knew my father had really been looking forward to it. It was all that he wanted to talk about.

Religious debate was the World Cup or the Super Bowl of my village. Debate was not really how issues were settled—it was how we were entertained!

In the middle of our village, there was a small square that had a shady tree in the center and patches of grass here and there. This was the main "ring" for debates between visiting monks. It was in this way that the teachings of our religion reached our village.

Such debates made quite an impression on me. When I was alone in the mountains, I would sometimes pretend I was in a debate with another monk. I would use any opportunity of silence and solitude to pretend that I was an enlightened debater who could capture the imagination of the masses with my intellect.

In a Tibetan debate, the challenging monk stands to his feet and makes his argument, while the defending monk remains in a seated position, carefully listening to the points of the challenger. In this current village debate, as I attempted to look through the crowd, I could not see the two lama teachers enter the square—but I heard the debate as it started. A general buzz rose from the crowd at the front. I could taste the excitement and I desperately wanted a front-row seat.

On the far side of the square, I finally found a small gap between two elderly monks from the monastery. It was the perfect spot. I could see and hear everything that was going on.

The challenging monk, who had been standing, walked away with long struts and then turned in mid-stride like a kung fu warrior, assuming a combatant stance. A string of beads hung from his right hand. He leaned down to speak directly into the face of the defending monk, who was perfectly calm and still.

"Which is more beneficial? To follow the enlightened or the writings of the enlightened?" As he finished his question, he brought his two arms together in a whip-like manner that made a loud clapping thud, immediately demanding the audience's attention.

Sitting on the ground and tapping his hands on the dirt, the defending monk responded, "I accept. Both are demanded of us by the Buddha and both are necessary. What do we know of the Buddha that is not written? What school of Buddhism relies only on the sangha?" (The *sangha* refers to those in monastic community.)

This was not a typical debate. Tibetan debates have clearly defined rules: the challenger makes statements and the defender sitting on the ground either accepts or does not accept the statement as a matter of truth and then challenges that the statement be backed up with logic and scripture. But this debate was something more. The defender was challenging the challenger. It was a clash of two great minds, and it was fascinating.

Without missing his cue, it seemed that the defender had now walked right into the trap that had been laid for him. The challenger continued, "Didn't the Buddha say, 'My teaching is not a philosophy—but the result of direct experience?' Didn't he say, 'My teaching is a means of practice, not something to hold on to or worship?' The Buddha taught his disciples so that they could teach us. Our belief is best passed down to us by those who have lived the experience, not by those who have merely studied it. How can you study and explain the color blue if you have never seen the color blue?"

Still sitting on the ground, the defender made a big circle in the air with his hand. "I do not accept. A good disciple will write down what he has learned to share with others. His writings ensure the longevity of the experience for others. To find the path for one's own sake is a good and noble thing. To find the path and make a map for others to find, as well, is even better. Is it not better to bless others rather than only yourself?"

The defending monk had not needed to end his question with a clap. His point had been made loud and clear. The crowd shifted its attention to the standing monk. How would he respond to that?

The debate started to get heated. The challenging monk raised his voice and demanded to know, "Are you saying that we do not have a choice? The only way that we can find treasures is by following maps? Has the Buddha died? Has he not returned to us? Are we so much in need of writings because your faith in the reincarnate Buddha is lacking?"

With that, he clapped again and held out his left hand as a gesture for the defender to respond. But before the seated monk could answer, the challenger interrupted him and continued, "I do not accept. What good are the writings of a teacher if we have access to the teacher? Writings are only a temporary vehicle from one shore to another when we are in absence of the teacher. As the Buddha said, 'Only a fool would carry a raft around after he had already reached the other shore of liberation.'"

This was getting good. It was the lively debate my father had been waiting for. The debaters' voices were growing loud, but still there was nothing threatening or violent in their tone. The primary purpose of their debate was to sharpen and hone their skills for defending the Buddhist faith and way of life through logic and truth. The topics were always varied, but purposeful.

The sitting monk calmly pointed to his head and said, "I must rely only on what I have learned, and I have learned through my experiences, the experiences of others, and the education of my mind. Buddha told me to think, so I think. Buddha told me to read, so I read. Buddha told me to pray, so I pray. To overemphasize any of these is to neglect all of them. Buddha taught the Four Reliances: First, to rely on the spirit and meaning of the teachings, not the words. Second, to rely on the teachings, not the personality of the teacher. Third, to rely on real wisdom, not superficial interpretation. And fourth, to rely on the essence of a pure mind—not judgmental perceptions."

To that, the challenger yelled out, "But you are ignoring Buddha when he said, 'Do not accept anything simply because it has been said by your teacher, or because it has been written in your sacred books, or because it has been believed by many, or because it has been handed down by your ancestors. Accept and live only according to what will enable you to see truth face-to-face.' What better way to find truth than to directly learn from those who have experienced it?"

The defender looked up and responded, "The reason is not established. What is your proof? You will not be punished because of your ignorance. You will be punished by it."

I sat there for several hours listening to them go at it. Hearing these two wise lamas debate each other about the pillars and virtues of Buddhism was one of the best educations I could ever get. In the end, I do not know who the winner was, but both monks were celebrated with free food from the village for their effort to make us all better in defending our faith and way of life.

Only a few years later, I would enter fully into my own quest for enlightenment. I could not know then the surprising ways in which my journey would lead me to encounter Truth face-to-face—and the far-reaching consequences of discovering that Truth....

A gathering of Tibetan monks.

Tibetan women with prayer beads and prayer wheels.

A young monk spinning a prayer wheel.

Large prayer wheels.

Giant Buddha statue.

Part One:
Learning the Ways of Buddha

1

BORN IN THE MOUNTAINS OF TIBET

I was born in a small mountain village in Jichu Township, in the same Chinese province where the Dalai Lama came from. I became a Buddhist monk when I was given as a gift by my parents to the local Tibetan Buddhist temple at about the age of fifteen. From my earliest memory, I had always identified as a monk. I did not know how else to refer to myself. I did not have any other identity. I had been following the divine ways of Buddha my entire life.

My family comes from a long line of Tibetan Buddhists. It is in my blood. It is my heritage. For generations, our family has served in the highest levels of the monasteries and has taught others how to follow the ways of Buddha.

In Tibet, everything revolves around Tibetan Buddhism, and no decisions are made without the lama's authority. A *lama* is a revered spiritual leader, but they are more than leaders. Many are considered to be the reincarnation of great sages and teachers from previous generations. A lama, whose title is directly translated as the "superior one," is the cornerstone of the Tibetan people. They are the village magistrates, the family counselors, the teachers in the monasteries, the national political leaders, and those who hold similar significant roles.

Lamas play a big part in the everyday lives of the people. For families like the one I was born into, they function like a Christian pastor, but they are much more than that. They often name babies and incorporate their own names into the names they give. The greater the influence of the lama, the more children who walk around with their name. I received the name *Tenzin* from a senior lama that my family followed. The name comes from the fourteenth Dalai Lama. Because he became extremely famous, many Tibetans today have the same name.

I was the sixth and final child born of my mother. Before this, she had given birth to three other boys and two girls, although one of my sisters died at birth. I was the baby of the family, and I felt I had a special relationship with my mother. I do not know if this was true or not, but I always had the feeling that I was her favorite child. My older siblings constantly accused me of this, and in many ways, I believed it. I was able to spend more time with my mother than my brothers and sisters were because they were often strapped with daily chores that I did not have to carry out—although, later, I was required to work in the fields.

Mother always kept special sweets hidden throughout the house for me to eat. When no one else was looking, she would tap me on the shoulder, point to an old pot or bag, and tell me to look under it. When I did, I would find a piece of candy or a treat. As soon as I snatched it up, she would place her index finger in front of her lips to indicate that I should be quiet about it so no one else would know.

Consisting of only five children, our family was considered to be a bit smaller than most. My mother came from a more typical-sized Tibetan family. She had eleven brothers and sisters, and she was one of the younger children, so there was a huge age gap between my grandparents and me. They were deceased before I really got to know much about them.

Outside of the Tibetan monasteries, which carefully record everything that happens in the lives of certain prominent lamas, there are not many ways to trace the family lineage of everyday working people like my grandparents. I do not know where they came from, when they married, or other details about their lives. In Tibet, mothers and fathers really do not talk much about family history or genealogy unless it pertains to a family member who was a well-known religious monk or leader.

Our village was made up of about thirty families who lived on the side of a mountain. Today, it is still a typical Tibetan mountain village. The terrain is harsh and the climate is dry. In Tibet, the air is thinner than in other places in China because of the altitude. Monks who visit the village from the basin can easily find themselves sick in the first couple of hours because of the low level of oxygen.

Looking out from my village, there are nothing but brown, sandy mountains for as far as the eye can see. There are few rivers and almost no trees. During the harsh winter months, sand storms blow from side to side, and there is almost no sign of green life. We do not have a lot of flowers or grass. There are only a few small, thin, sparsely planted trees that are dotted with a few green leaves when the spring rains come—if they come.

When I was growing up in our village, the main crops were wheat and highland barley. We also grew radishes and potatoes when the weather permitted. Unlike the bigger cities of China, my village was free from pollution. We did most of our production and farming naturally and wasted very little. During the day, you could see for miles around. And at night, it seemed as if you could see every star in the sky.

My home was built from local brown clay mud and designed in the same way that Tibetans have been making their homes for thousands of years. The light khaki color of our house matched the surrounding dry, sandy, mountain range. Because trees are scarce, we had to use dry dung as fuel for our fires. We collected manure from our livestock while it was still warm and soft, added straw to it, mixed it up with our hands, and made round patties. Then we put these big, round, wet patties on the outside of our homes so that they could dry in the sun.

The interior of our home was characteristically Tibetan, as well—designed as one large room where everyone lived. The kitchen, the living room, and the bedroom were all located in one main area. In the center of our home was a black, iron, pot belly stove that we used for cooking our meals, warming our tea, and heating our home in the winter. During the day, we would sit near the stove on an elevated wooden structure that turned into our bed at night. We all slept together on thin, flat mattresses around the big black stove.

The elevated wooden structure was also the location where I was born. Women in my village do not go to hospitals to give birth to their children. It is tradition for a local midwife to come and sit with the mothers throughout the birthing process, and everyone prays that there will be no serious complications.

My mother lost only one of her babies giving birth in the traditional Tibetan way, and she survived that ordeal, so we were one of the fortunate families. Usually, when a mother has complications during the birthing process, she loses not only her baby, but also her own life. However, my mother was a tough woman, and everyone in the village knew and respected her. She had a quiet strength that exuded from her personality. Her strong presence did not need to be announced. It was just there.

My mother did all of the hard, laborious work to keep our family going. She cared for the animals. She plowed the fields and pulled the harvest. She ground the wheat by hand and made the bread. She butchered the animals and cooked the meat. She cleaned the house and cared for the children.

When I was born near the black, iron stove, it was 1969, soon after China's Mao Zedong took over Tibet. The Dalai Lama gave orders for Tibetans to accept the occupation of Mao Zedong, but then he fled to India to save his own life. He left the Tibetan people to suffer under the weight of his decision.

During this time, people were dying from starvation all over the country due to the effects of the "Great Leap Forward" in China (1958–1961), a failed social and economic campaign by the Communist Party. However, the Tibetan people have never been rich, so they were used to surviving off of the land and triumphing over harsh conditions. The Chinese people did not fare so well. Tens of millions of them died during those years.

In many ways, those times were not easy for anyone—neither the Chinese nor the Tibetans.

2

A DEVOUT MOTHER

My earliest memories involve my mother praying and teaching me Buddhist scriptures. She spent a lot of time trying to encourage me to memorize the holy scripture of Buddha.

I remember waking up in the early morning hours as a small child and seeing my mother already praying to the different spirits in our home. We were always short on food, and my mother wanted to keep us nourished, so she attempted to appease the gods with hopes of granting us better crops and more livestock.

If praying in this way could have provided more food for her children, we would have been the fattest children in the village! She used every ounce of her ability and energy to appease the gods so that her children would be safe and healthy. However, no matter how much she prayed, it never seemed to be enough.

My mother was a petite, well-rounded woman—and as solid as a barrel from her head to her feet. Her long, pitch-black hair was always tightly pulled back and braided into a ponytail. Her dark hair shone and reflected glimmers from the sun.

My mother did not have a wardrobe of clothes to choose from. She had one main outfit that she would wear every day during the summer and a much thicker one that she would wear every day in the winter. She dressed in a black *chuba*, which is a long, sheepskin coat made from thick, Tibetan wool that is worn by many Tibetans. My mother's chuba was bordered with big, bold, colorful patterns of brilliant blue, orange, and tan. The collar, which stretched from her neck all the way to the tip of her shoulder, was sky blue. On the forearms of the sleeves were matching blue markings. She often wore a red fabric belt as a sash around her waist, which could give the impression that her long coat was actually two separate pieces. To me, it was as if my mother's clothing was a part of her and she was a part of her clothing. The two seemed inseparable in my mind.

Like everyone else in our village, we had a picture of the Dalai Lama on our wall—even though it was illegal to do so in China—with holy scripture written in Tibetan script. The picture and scripture were covered by glass and encased in an ornate, golden frame. Draped over the frame was a white scarf, which is a typical homage in our culture for an honored guest. This signified that the spirit of the holy lama of Tibet would forever be welcomed in our home.

The picture of the Dalai Lama was there when I woke up and it was there when I went to sleep. He was always watching me. For many who know little about the Dalai Lama, it might seem that seeing his face would have invoked ideas of peace and tranquility for me, but it did not. His picture brings peace only for those who do not fully understand the darkness of Tibetan Buddhism, which is different from all the other forms of Buddhism.

In Tibetan Buddhism, there is a strong incorporation of Hinduism that lingers. This does not exist as strongly in other expressions of Buddhism that you might find in Japan, Thailand, or New York. For instance, on the wooden pillars of the door at our home, there was an image of a man-sized monkey with an evil, angry, red face, holding a sword. In front of the monkey, on her knees, was a woman who had had her throat slit by the monkey. Blood gushed from the sides of the woman's mouth and poured down her neck. The monkey was peering over her shoulder showing his jagged teeth. He was holding the woman's head by her hair, and her eyes expressed a look of terror in the knowledge that she was about to die.

That sight might be incredibly disturbing to most outsiders, but for Tibetans, the gore was very natural. Every village in my area had icons or pictures of the Tibetan monkey god, Pha Trelgen Changchup Sempa, painted on its walls and homes. In the Tibetan form of Buddhism, the monkey god is the most important figure. He is given the same level of recognition as Buddha, because it is believed that the Tibetan people are his descendants. It is thought that in the beginning, the world was covered by a great flood. As the water started to dry up, there was a union between the monkey god, who was in the Tibetan mountains meditating, and a woman who approached him wanting to have intercourse with him.

At first, the monkey refused to have sex with the woman, but she threatened to have intercourse with a demon instead and give birth to many demons that would roam the world and wreak havoc on everyone. The meditating monkey eventually gave in to the woman's demands and requested that Avalokitesvara, the reincarnation of the Dalai Lama, perform a marriage ceremony between them.

The woman gave birth to baby monkeys who multiplied so greatly that the food of the forest could not sustain them. Avalokitesvara taught them agricultural skills so they could eat the fruit of their labor instead of food that had been foraged.

Soon the monkeys began to lose their hair and their tails. The monkeys built on the concepts they had been shown, and they started to use clothing and construct houses. They formed a civilization of "evolved" monkeys who would later be known as the Tibetan people.

This background is essential for understanding Tibetan Buddhism, because it is where the Dalai Lama comes in and how he is connected to Tibet in a way that he is not connected to India or Nepal—the birthplace of Buddhism. According to Tibetan belief, the Dalai Lama is the reincarnation of the leaders before him, all the way back to Avalokitesvara and the monkey god—the same monkey god that was holding a knife to the throat of the terrified woman in the picture that I saw every day.

The reincarnation of the Dalai Lama is at the heart of the Tibetan people. The Dalai Lama is a *tulku*, which is a reincarnate custodian of Tibetan Buddhist teachings and authority. Tulkus are unique to Tibet. They are anointed from birth as the reincarnation of a former ruler. They are then trained as children by students of their predecessor. Before a tulku dies, they speak in detail about their death, reincarnation, and rebirth.

Thus, the monkey god is honored and venerated as the father of the Tibetan people, and my mother was putting all of her eggs into the basket of the religion that deified the monkey god and the reincarnation of the one who performed the marriage of the monkey to the evil woman.

If my mother's prayers were ever really heard by the monkey god or the Buddha, there were never any signs of it.

3

AN OVERPOWERING FATHER

The darkness of my childhood did not originate from the paintings of Hindu demons I saw every day. It came from the early days of seeing my mother suffer at the hands of my father, a stern man who towered over her.

My father was born a middle child, with two older brothers and two younger sisters. He grew up poor but devoted to Buddha. His hands were rough and coarse from laboring in the fields day after day and working the ropes with the livestock. Arduous work in those fields had made him tough and solid. His voice was deep and scratchy, mainly due to the calls he made every day. Tibetans do not rely on phones; instead, when they want to call or send a message to someone in a different village, they climb to the top of a mountain and make a loud "hooting" sound to the next mountain. When their hooting call is answered, they shout information to be passed along until a message has been delivered. This can happen from mountain to mountain and from village to village.

There was a trick to this method of calling. One did not simply yell loudly and expect the message to carry. A basic understanding of the workings of acoustics was needed. The voice had to be projected in such a way that the shape of the mountains could be used to bounce the noise into the pocket of where you wanted the message to be carried. My father was recognized for being able to belt out a loud hooting call that would bounce around the mountains for several seconds.

In addition to his calling ability, my father was known for his love of rice wine. The rice wine in our village was usually homemade. It was a clear liquid with a straw-yellow tint to it, was poured from a diesel container, and had the smell of jet fuel.

I can't really say specifically what my father did day after day, because he was largely absent. When he was around the house, he mainly prayed, smoked his pipe, and got drunk—and it was when he was drunk that he would beat my mother. After spending the day out in the fields and drinking rice wine, he would stumble home and break out in fits of rage against her. The woman who had spent all day praying to Buddha and the half dozen additional Tibetan gods whose images were placed around our home would then receive a beating from her husband.

He would beat her for not doing her job the right way or not preparing his food in the correct manner. The reasons were all different and yet the same. His excuses for beating her were always lame and irrational.

I would cringe for her. Although she was a stout and strong woman, she was still not able to ward off the poundings he dealt her. She would beg him to stop, but he would continue on.

There was nowhere for us children to hide from this situation because we all lived in the same room. We would quietly sob for our mother and silently beg the gods to stop my father from beating her. We would never speak louder than a whisper for fear that our father's anger would turn against us. Tears flowed down our faces and we winced at each swat my father took at my mother as if the hand that came crashing down from on high were coming down on us. We empathized with every slap she endured.

We all knew what his beatings felt like. There were times when he was angry with us and would rip off his belt and swing it around in the air, hitting us anywhere the belt chose to land. We would cry out to our mother to come and save us. Whenever possible, she would try to intervene when she knew we had reached our limit. There were many times when she would put her own body in between us and our father to try to convince him to stop beating us. She was the one we would call on when we were being beaten—but she had no one to call on to help her.

Our mother could call out to our gods, but in the end, only the "god of exhaustion" would coincidentally answer her prayers. After my father finally got tired out and stopped beating her, he would fall asleep. We would then try to crawl up and cling to our mother. We would move to her slowly so as to not make a noise that would wake our father back up. I can remember feeling her body shake from the intense emotional and physical trauma. Even after she stopped crying, her body would shiver as it gasped for more oxygen. We would not say anything to her, and she would not use words to attempt to comfort us. Our presence was all we had to communicate with one another.

I never heard my parents say they loved each other, and I never saw them show any affection for one another. In our Tibetan culture, words or physical displays of affection are considered to be shameful. Consequently, I spent my entire childhood never hearing the words "I love you." Our family was not strange in this way. I do not believe that there was even one child in my entire village who ever heard the word *love*. Somehow, I understood the concept of love. I knew what it meant. But I never actually heard it expressed.

Those who are not really familiar with Buddhism might think that Tibetan Buddhism teaches love as one of its main tenants of faith, but it does not. Anyone who would argue that Buddhism is about love does not know the true story of Buddha's family.

Buddha's real name was Prince Siddhartha Gautama. He was born the only son of a royal family more than twenty-five hundred years ago in modern-day Nepal. He married his cousin, Princess Yasodhara, the daughter of his father's sister, and they had a baby boy. The night Prince Siddhartha planned to sneak out of the royal castle to chase his dream of finding enlightenment, he was told about the birth of his son, to which he replied, "An impediment has come into being, a bond has come into being."[1] Prince Siddhartha's son was given the name Rahula, which means "fetter" or "impediment." A physical fetter is a metal cuff that is chained around the ankles of a prisoner.

From a very young age, Tibetan Buddhists are taught that showing love and affection toward one's family members is a fetter, or impediment, to achieving enlightenment. In order to attain enlightenment, which is the greatest quest for any Tibetan, you must cut off your feelings of love and emotion toward those who are closest to you.

When Prince Siddhartha left the castle, he did so under the darkness of night because he was afraid his wife would cry and beg him to stay. He was emotionless and severed all ties with his family. Although he was the only son of his father and had a wife and son, he abandoned his responsibilities to his family to seek what he thought was good for himself.

When Rahula grew a little older, many nights, he would cry out for his father. Word was sent all around the kingdom to let the prince know that his son wanted only to see his father. When Rahula was about six or seven years old, the Buddha returned, but not to stay. Rahula was fascinated to finally see his father. He was filled with excitement and is recorded as saying, "[Father], even your shadow is pleasing to me."[2]

But Prince Siddhartha remained unfazed by the love of his son, treating both his wife and his son with extreme sterility. He was holy and they were not. He was the Buddha, and to show emotion to them would have weakened his enlightenment.

---

1. Viggo Fausbøll, *Buddhist Birth Stories: Or, Jātaka Tales*, vol. 1, trans. Thomas William Rhys Davids (London: Trübner & Co, 1880), 79, http://www.gutenberg.org/files/51880/51880-0.txt.
2. See http://religiondocbox.com/Buddhism/71771218-Rahula-thera-siddhatta-and-yasodhara-only-son.html, page 3.

Therefore, I want you to understand that for my father to show love and devotion to my mother or me and my siblings would have been antithetical to Tibetan Buddhism. Unselfish love for others is incompatible with it.

Buddhism teaches us to sacrifice ourselves and to rid ourselves of our ego, but before we can fully give up our inner attachments and abandon ourselves, we must give up our external attachments and abandon others.

In this way, perhaps our father's violence was a strange, unrecognizable act of love. By abusing us and showing no emotion toward us, he was helping us to more easily detach ourselves from him in our quest for enlightenment. Or maybe that is a stretch on my part in a vain attempt to attribute love to an overbearing and abusive father.

4

THE ALL-SEEING EYE

It was not just the pictures in our house that I thought were watching me 24-7. The eyes of the Buddha were always on me as well.

In modern-day China, cameras are everywhere—the government is always watching its citizens. There are currently 176 million surveillance cameras, with another 500 million on the way to be installed in 2020. That is almost one camera for every two citizens.[3]

These cameras help the Chinese government to have an all-seeing eye, enabling it to answer questions like: "Where are people going?" "Who are they talking to?" "What are they doing?" "Where are they working?" If you know the government is watching your every move, then maybe you will not do anything wrong.

In Tibet, we have an ancient system that is reminiscent of these surveillance cameras. It is called the "Third Eye of Buddha." The Third Eye of Buddha is the all-seeing eye that watches everything and everyone. As a

3. Ryan Grenoble, "Welcome to the Surveillance State: China's AI Cameras See All," December 12, 2017, https://www.huffingtonpost.com/entry/china-surveillance-camera-big-brother_us_5a2ff4dfe4b01598ac484acc.

child, playing outside, I was aware of the Third Eye of Buddha. I knew that if I did anything wrong, disobeyed the village lama, or did not pray enough, this all-seeing Eye would witness it, and I would experience bad *karma*.

Karma is central to Tibetan Buddhism. This force encompasses any thought, word, action, or deed that one creates. Karma itself is neither positive nor negative; it just exists, and the all-seeing Eye observes everything, meting out to people the consequences of their actions, whether good or bad, by the state of their existence in their next reincarnation.

There is bad karma—things that can bring suffering or future reincarnation to a lower state, but it is not "evil karma." There is no such thing as evil karma. In Tibetan Buddhism, there is no "good and evil," as in the Christian sense—there is only positive and negative karma, or things that will cause suffering or blessing in the next life. Something that is evil by the simple fact of being a sin does not exist.

Karma is like a point-based system—sort of like a bank account. Your bank account is either positive or negative. If your karma is positive, that is good for getting benefits and having less suffering in the next life. If it is negative, that is bad for the consequences you will experience in next life.

With karma, none of us has a beginning or an ending. We are all a part of a cyclic existence that goes around and around unless we become enlightened.

When I was young, the straw would be gathered from the fields and spread across the ground to dry. My father would make a large circle with white paint, and the straw would be placed on top of this circle. One day, I asked him what the white circle meant, and he told me it was the circle of life. All things feed off of one another. The animals feed off of the straw and we feed off of the animals. When we die, our bodies will return to the ground for the straw to feed off of our bodies. In this way, our bodies are eternal. They are never destroyed; they only change form.

Our actions are eternal as well. Things that we do today create events for tomorrow—and tomorrow is not limited to this lifetime. We are a lifetime of endless lifetimes, and any successive lifetime can be affected by something we do or do not do today.

The concept of karma was taught to me as a child to keep me from doing anything my mother did not want me to do. My mother discouraged me from having bad thoughts, skipping prayer, or neglecting my duties as a Buddhist. If I did, Buddha would know. His all-seeing eye saw everything. I could not hide. In Tibetan Buddhism, people live in constant fear of the actions they take, knowing that the all-seeing Eye never sleeps. The Eye is always awake—watching you and knowing your deepest, darkest thoughts.

The Tibetan eyes of judgment are everywhere. Almost every main gate, wall, tower, and statue of Buddha in Tibet is adorned with eyes that are unnerving from the very first moment you see them. Shrines built to Buddha, called *stupas*, are usually towering structures that hold relics or the remains of a Buddhist monk or nun, and are used as a place of prayer and meditation. All four sides of the main towers are painted with giant eyes. These represent omnipresent observation and remind people that there is no way to avoid being seen.

Our village stupa is concrete grey, with four layers of a square foundation built one on top of the other, similar to a wedding cake. At the top is a rounded bronze statue. The entire shape of the stupa represents Buddha, crowned and sitting in meditation posture on a throne. His crown is the top of the spire, his head is the square at the spire's base, and his eyes peer out to watch your every move.

Thus, a sense of bondage permeates Tibetan culture through the all-seeing Eye; people feel that no one can ever escape its relentless observation. Whenever I played outside, I would be distracted by this unsettling feeling from time to time—but never for long. I always had the knowledge in the back of my mind that everything I did and every thought I had was being watched. That knowledge controlled my behavior and never let me wander too far from Buddhism.

If you take a close look at the eyes of a statue of Buddha, you will see that they are not fully open. They are only half open in order to indicate that the third eye of Buddha might not see everything clearly in the spiritual, but can see perfectly in the natural.

I did not feel my mother had anything to hide from the all-seeing eyes of Buddha. She would walk around the stupa every day for hours, praying and building up positive karma that would benefit her in the future—either in this life or in the one to come. I was certain that Buddha's eyes were getting tired of seeing her there every day. They needed someone new to look at.

It was always amazing to me that my mother didn't grow any thinner from all of her long prayer walks around that stupa. But if those eyes had any fairness in them at all, if they truly saw everything, then they would have known that my mother needed her burdens to be lifted.

My mother needed protection against my father. She should have been able to obtain security for her children. She deserved to be comforted for the sacrifices she made. But the all-seeing Eye of Buddha seemed to be silent. Powerless. Dead.

The all-seeing Eye did not give hope in exchange for devotion. Instead it gave only exhaustion and fear.

5

THE CHILDHOOD OF BUDDHA

"Queen Maya ruled over a small kingdom in the north of India, and one night she had a very strange dream. Her dream would change the world." My mother's voice was soft and animated. By the time I was nine years old, she was almost sixty, so she was not able to chase me around the yard and play games like the younger mothers in our village did with their children. But no one could tell a story like my mother!

"One night, the queen was sleeping when she dreamed of a brilliant light shining down from the sky. In the rays of the blinding light was a majestic white elephant with massive white tusks descending down to her."

Every Buddhist child is told the story of this great white elephant. It is a powerful image that can be found as the centerpiece of art in Buddhist culture.

"The elephant was this big," my mother said as she spread out her arms as far as they would go. "And it was pure white, like the fresh snow on the mountaintops of our village mountains."

My mother then told me how the elephant melted into the queen's body. "At that moment, the queen woke up. She ran to tell the king about her dream, and together they ran to the wise men of the court, who told them that her dream was great fortune. The wise men told the queen that she had been chosen to give birth to a great son, and he would change the world."

That son was Prince Siddhartha, who would later become Buddha. Siddhartha was actually born into a Hindu family and was a practicing Hindu his entire life. When Siddhartha was born, a *Brahmin*, or Hindu priest, prophesied to the king that this son would one day be a great king, but he would need to be sheltered from the outside world so that he would not leave the kingdom.

Siddhartha's father, King Suddhodana, created a paradise for his son within the walls of the kingdom. It was a place of peace and calm. It was a home of wealth and happiness. Nothing bad ever happened there.

As a little boy, listening to the life of Buddha sounded like heaven to me. He had everything that I dreamed of having. He had a father who loved him and friends to play with. He lived in a castle and had plenty of food to eat every day. He was protected from the evil, cruel world.

"As a child, Siddhartha did not see anyone sick, hurt, or die," my mother said with a smile on her face. I rarely saw my mother smile. With her harsh life, smiling did not come easy for her. I think that my mother sometimes told me the story of Buddha's childhood as a kind of escape from her own reality. In a strange way, relating the story of Buddha's early life brought her a little sense of security.

The environment of sterility and safety that shaped Prince Siddhartha's life would lead to his famous "Four Sights." The Four Sights of Buddha are four things Siddhartha saw that started his entire journey to enlightenment and led to what we now call Buddhism. The young prince did not venture outside of his castle walls until he was about twenty-nine years old. When he did, his first sight was of an old man, and he witnessed the effects of age. His good friend Channa, who had accompanied him, told him that old age happens to everyone. In Siddhartha's sheltered life, he had never seen an old person before, and the experience traumatized him.

For his second sight, he saw a sick person. This shocked him, also, because he had never before seen a sick person. No ill person was ever allowed into the royal palace.

For his third sight, Siddhartha saw a dead body. He had never seen or even heard of anyone dying. His father had made sure that the sick, old, and dying were sent out of the palace before Siddhartha could see them. Again, Siddhartha's good friend Channa explained that death is inevitable for everyone. Everyone dies.

After seeing these three examples of human frailty, Siddhartha saw a fourth sight—a monk who had devoted his life to finding the cause of human suffering. The prince then determined to do the very thing that his father had feared for his entire life that he might—follow the example of the monk and find the end to human suffering.

When Siddhartha returned to the palace, a group of dancing girls was arranged for him, but their beauty and dancing did not make him forget the suffering he had witnessed. After that day, he decided to leave and live the life of a monk, never to return as the wealthy prince who would one day inherit his father's kingdom.

My mother told me these stories with great enthusiasm, as if she had been there to witness all of the Four Sights with Siddhartha himself. These stories were important to her and our family as the cornerstone of the Tibetan people.

The Four Sights led Siddhartha to have huge questions that his religion did not and could not answer. He did not leave his comfortable life as the pampered prince to train as a priest. From reading his writings my entire life, I have found no evidence that he set out to start a new religion or become a famous teacher. He left because the things that he had seen greatly disturbed him and left him with unanswered questions. He saw pain and suffering and wanted to know why and how to end it.

My mother understood suffering and she believed that Siddhartha had found the answer to ending it. From the prayers that she prayed so fervently every single day, I know that she, too, wanted to end suffering. She desperately wanted to believe that all of the causes of suffering she saw every day could cease: the poverty and violence of the Tibetan people, the abuse from my father, the death of her daughter as an infant, the absence of running water and electricity, the lack of shoes for me to wear and the lack of clothes to keep me warm when the cold weather came.

My mother did not have the luxury of leaving her children to fend for themselves, as Siddhartha had done to his wife and son. She was committed to ending our misery more than she was committed to ending her own, but most of the time, she felt that she was failing at both.

She looked to Buddha for answers.

As a child, observing my mother, I could not help but see that whatever answers she found in Buddhism to end the pain seemed to be temporary. Very temporary.

Siddhartha started out his journey on a quest for answers. He began with questions and used Hinduism as his initial vehicle to search for the answers to those questions. Like Siddhartha, I, too, had many questions. Buddhism was my vehicle for searching for answers through enlightenment. But my eventual conclusions would not be accepted by those who follow Buddha. In fact, what I would find would bring even more pain to my mother and almost cost me my life.

6
TIBETAN HOLY DAYS

Although village life was not easy while I was growing up, I do have a few childhood memories of enjoying Buddhist festivals. The festivities were always a great way to break up the monotony of working in the fields.

During planting and harvesttime, there was a lot of work to be done. We had oxen and sheep that needed to be tended to every day. If our oxen were not properly cared for, we would not have them for plowing and tilling during planting season and they would not be able to help us carry our crops back during harvesttime.

While working in the fields, I would dream of the next holiday. Tibetan holidays are a time when everyone eats, shares food, and relaxes.

The tension in our family would ease for a while and our problems seemed to be momentarily forgotten. During the festivals in Tibet, there was so much leisure time that it allowed everyone to visit with their families and enjoy some carefree days.

Tibetan celebrations are an explosion of colors. Because our mountain villages are mostly grey and brown, we crave the pigmentation of bright colors. Festivities give the people an escape from their monotone lives, enabling them to step out of the grey-brown canvas of the Tibetan mountains. Festive reds, blues, and yellows help to break through the choking sand and dung patties and breathe life back into their lives. Colorful clothing and banners during Buddhist holidays created the feeling of celebration.

As a little boy, it was always hard for me to sleep on the night before a big festival. My mind would race, thinking about all of the bright banners decorating the village. I would also be excited about the sweets I knew were coming. What's more, I would be allowed to run around the village freely with my friends and not have to worry about work. I didn't have any toys to play with, such as you can find in China today. Toys were implements I would make myself. I often fashioned simple slingshots that I could use to hunt birds with rocks. I would not necessarily eat the birds—I would just hunt them and kill them for the sport. My friends and I had a special game where we would make a circle and place big rocks in the middle, and then we would attempt to knock the stones out of the circle by throwing other rocks at them. If there was nothing else to do, I would find old carcasses of animals and try to put the bones back together to recreate the skeleton of the animal.

I didn't recognize it then, but I really had several festivals to look forward to. One of the big celebrations that excited me was the Yogurt Festival. The celebration would happen at the end of the summer after the hottest days of the year when there was no escaping from the intensity of the sun. The summer heat made it difficult to carry out regular farm duties, so many families attempted to do as little work as possible to conserve their energy. However, families like mine had no choice. We had to work to survive—no matter how hot it got. During this time, we would not see or hear from the monks in our village. They would retreat into the monastery and stay inside for about a month. They tried not to walk around or expend any energy. A bit of fear would sweep over the village in their absence, because it was believed that the monks knew the secrets to keeping the demons at bay. Bad things could happen to the village people if the monks were to stay away too long.

It was the people's job to look after the monks in the village and take care of their needs. So, at the end of the summer, when the temperatures were less intense, the villagers would put together a Yogurt Festival where cool, soothing yogurt was offered to the monks as a refreshing treat. The playing of clashing cymbals, bells, and drums lasted all day long in order to scare away the demons and bring out the blessing of the monks. Friends and family members would dress up like demons to imitate the devils we were trying to avoid. My father assisted in getting the massive, ornate rugs that were hung from the mountainsides as decorations, and my mother helped to make the yogurt with the other village women.

The yogurt is a sweet-and-sour concoction, and I secretly didn't want to give it to the monks—I wanted to keep it all for myself. However, I knew that if we didn't give it, there might be a chance that the demons would see an open door in our house and attack us without the spiritual protection of the monks. Nevertheless, one day, I asked my mother why we couldn't just keep the yogurt for ourselves. So many of the other villagers had made plenty of yogurt to feed to the monks. Surely, they would not miss ours. That is when she told me the story of the demonic underworld full of hungry ghosts. "One day, one of Buddha's disciples named Moggallana came to him and asked the Buddha how he could help his mother, who was in a place of torment called Avici, which is one of the lowest realms of hell. Avici is a place where the suffering never ends. Those who live there are tormented by fire and evil spirits, and they are forever hungry."

At that time, I knew only parts of the story. Hearing my mother tell it made it more real for me.

"Do you know why the disciple's mother was sent to Avici?" she asked me. I shook my head. "Because she was greedy with her food. She allowed monks to pass by without giving them anything to eat. Anyone who withholds food from the monks will one day find themselves reincarnated in Avici, where people have ravenous appetites but nothing to eat. They are tormented day and night."

In the story, the Buddha tells his disciple that he can offer a tray of food to the monks when they return from their summer retreat. This will prompt them to pray for you in a way that can benefit you and several of your generations from experiencing Avici. When the disciple fed the monks a hearty meal, his mother was lifted out of hell and reincarnated as a dog in a rich family. The disciple was then instructed to give both food and fine new robes to five hundred monks, and this elevated his mother's status back to a human being when she reincarnated again.

The tormented demons in hell are remembered every year during the Ghost Festival, also known as the festival of the Beating Ghost, which takes place during the full moon. The gates of hell were opened up, and the dead who are suffering are allowed to roam about looking for food and entertainment. If they do not find it, they are free to torment their family members who do not show love and respect to them.

Monks and followers often wear demonic masks and roam the streets to remind people that demons are all around them during this time. Seats at the family dining table during meals and even at different events in the village are left empty for the dead who were roaming the earth. Food offerings are laid out at their places. Family members have been known to burn valuable items like money, cars, houses, and even servants in an attempt to appease the evil spirits roaming the earth during this time. The Ghost Festival is also when reincarnation takes place, so Tibetans try to get their ancestors a better position for reincarnation and also protect themselves from future hauntings and torment.

As a child, I thought of all the Buddhist holidays as a time of festivity, brilliant colors, food, and family. I always considered the festivals as a moment to stop suffering and to celebrate life and happiness. Yet as I reflected on the words of my mother, I started to understand that, in some way, each of our celebrations was motivated more by fear than by joy.

7

BUDDHA THE WARRIOR

Of all the Tibetan celebrations, there was one that I enjoyed above all others: the Archery Festival. I loved competing in this festival because it connected me with my warrior ancestors. The warrior ancestors of the Tibetan people struck fear in all the enemies that tried to conquer our mountain villages. Even today, the Chinese military does not want Tibetans to hold this competition without proper authorization. Our village rarely had any authorization. We were far from the seat of power and the mountains were high, insulating us. What the government did not know would not hurt them.

My father taught me that archery brought a sense of unity and served as an entertainment for the gods. If we were able to shoot straight and true with our bows, then the gods might smile on us and allow more rain for the harvest season or prevent hailstorms from destroying our crops. But if you lost during the competition—if you were not able to shoot straight and true with your arrows—it was usually an omen that sickness and poverty would fall upon you.

The Chinese occupiers who invaded Tibet would love for Tibetans to turn their Archery Festival into a sanitized sporting event, like the Olympics or Western competition, but it is not a basketball game or soccer tournament. It is considered holy and sacred. The archery competition was an ancient form of ushering boys into adulthood and connected us all to our common Buddhist history.

Tibetan archery goes back hundreds of years and harkens back to the days of our dominance over the Himalayan mountains. Our competitions usually took place at the end of the year and lasted for about five days. During that time, the family honor and wealth were on the line. The stakes were high, and it always gave me a bit of an adrenaline rush.

My father let me use his bow, but it was more than a bow. Traditional Tibetan bows are made of yak horn and bamboo with cordage of tightly braided strings of nettle fiber. My father's bow had about fifty to seventy pounds of draw. It was a carefully crafted weapon—and a symbol of our family pride.

Archers were the gladiators of the village, and it was a known fact that the best shooters received the prettiest brides. The best shooters won the most pride for their families to walk with respect through the village.

During the Archery Festival, we would make images of the gods from ghee[4] or yak butter and flowers. Many of the gods would be depicted with a bow in their hand, prepared to fight.

The original Buddha, Prince Siddhartha, came from a warrior clan. When Tibetans pray to Buddha, they refer to his family name, Shakyamuni, which denotes that Buddha belonged to the Sahkya clan, an elite warrior caste that ruled over portions of Nepal. Buddha was a trained warrior and fighter who had been systematically taught the skills of war in order to protect his kingdom. He completely mastered his combat training and even won his wife, Yasodhara, in an archery contest.

Buddha was a descendent of the Indo-Aryan race, which followed the Indo-Aryan gods of war, in addition to the Hindu gods. The Samyutta scripture tells us that Buddha's family line believed there was no other rule in life but to fight.

However, it can be very confusing for people to properly understand Tibetan Buddhism if they think Tibetans only follow Buddha. Each family follows at least ten gods, and those gods come from both Hinduism and traditional Tibetan religion. It can also be difficult to follow all of the stories of the different gods that Tibetans follow because there are more than thirty-three million gods in Hinduism alone! That is before we even explore the complexity of our traditional religions.

Buddha followed the Hindu religion, and the gods of the Hindu-Buddhist religion are armed with their own personal weapons and are masters of their own fighting skills. The most important god that Buddha would have been taught about in his youth was Vishnu. Vishnu, Brahma, and Shiva are considered to be the "holy trinity" of Hinduism. Vishnu is often depicted carrying his bow, named Sharanga, and Lord Shiva also carries a bow, named Pinaka. These bows were handed down to their reincarnations and carried mystical powers during battle (similar to something out of *The Lord of the Rings*). Even Krishna, who is the supreme god of Hinduism, used a bow in his battle against a demon named Shalva.

When people are only lightly exposed to Tibetan Buddhism, they sometimes walk away with the impression that all we do all day is pray.

---

4. "A semifluid clarified butter made especially in India," Merriam-Webster.com, 2018, http://www.merriam-webster.com.

They might not be aware of how much battle and combat are embedded into our religion. The Tibetan people have no problem with fighting. In fact, they quite enjoy it. The art of fighting with a bow and arrow goes to the heart of who Tibetans are as a people. From their roots, they have been known to be warriors.

To prepare for the archery competition, I would practice for hours every day after my work in the field. Winning an archery contest in a Tibetan village is the equivalent to winning the lottery. Your life would be better, your opportunities would be greater, and the villagers would respect you if you were known to be the best with a bow. Even if I was completely exhausted at the end of the day, I would find extra energy reserves for practicing with the bow until the sun went down and it became too dark to aim.

I dreamed about being a hero for my family and winning the top archery competitions in our area, but that dream would never come true. Even when I won the competitions I participated in, there always seemed to be something inside of my parents that kept them from truly celebrating. It was as if they had a secret they could not tell me.

They knew something about my life that I did not know, and it could not be changed no matter how many archery competitions I won or how famous I might become. My parents had made promises for my future, as I would soon find out.

8
MEETING A MONK

"Om mani padme hum," my mother chanted in prayer as we walked up to the altar.

"Om mani padme hum," I said in repetition after her. It was a phrase I had known since I was a child. Those might even have been the first words I said in a complete sentence.

My mother grasped a stack of small copper cups with one hand and a jug of water with the other. Gracefully, she poured the water into the first cup until it was almost full and then set down the water jug. After this, as she had done so many times before, she poured water from one cup into the next, lining them up on the altar in front of the meditating Buddha as she continued to chant "Om mani padme hum."

My mother was chanting the mantra of Chenrezig. Chenrezig is the embodiment of the compassion of all the Buddhas. He is the earthly manifestation of eternal Buddha and guards the portal between the historical Buddha and all future Buddhas. Chenrezig is the link between Siddhartha Buddha and the final Buddha, known as Maitreya. Prophecy states that Maitreya Buddha will reincarnate as a type of messiah to the world when everyone has forgotten the true teachings of Buddha.

The Chenrezig mantra is arguably the most important prayer in all of Tibetan Buddhism. All of the teachings of Buddha can be broken down into the six simple syllables of the Chenrezig mantra.

"Om mani padme hum" is not a phrase that can easily be translated into English. It is more complicated than just the words that are being said. It is a phrase that literally means "hail to the jewel in the lotus." The jewel in the lotus is a seed that is yet to grow and seeks to give birth, while the lotus is the fully developed flower representing true enlightenment. The phrase is sacred for our people and is thought to give power. It can be repeated out loud or silently to oneself. It has the same power whether it is vocalized or not. The Chenrezig mantra is believed to have power even if you simply read it, which is why the most famous Tibetan Buddhist monasteries have the words permanently etched into their walls or ceilings. When you walk, you can pray the mantra. When you pray, you can pray the mantra. When you eat, you can pray the mantra.

The Chenrezig mantra is written around the Mani wheel, which is a prayer wheel that you turn while you walk and pray. Inside of the prayer wheels are thousands of small, handwritten copies of the Chenrezig mantra. The Mani wheel represents the circle of life. You turn it as you pass by, praying the mantra, and it goes around and around, representing the repetitiveness of life.

"Om mani padme hum" my mother chanted again. I listened to her chant as if it were a sweet lullaby. After all, she had chanted her mantras to me to keep me from crying when I was a baby.

"Om mani padme hum," my mother softly repeated as she stepped back and placed her hands in front of her face in prayer. I glanced sideways at her and followed her lead as she prayed. My mother was clearly a holy woman and religiously devout. Sometimes I wanted to be like her. Sometimes I wanted to be more distant and practical like my father. But when I saw the peace that prayer brought to my mother, it made me happy. She had such a hard life otherwise. When she prayed, I could see that she was in the moment and the mantra gave her some kind of control over her life.

"When you pray, visualize that you have the spirit of Buddha in you," she once told me. "The Buddha of compassion can replace your thoughts. All of your pain and sadness will fall to the side when you reach inward and forget all else." She had a lot of pain and sadness, but it was never appropriate to talk about it. The mantra was the fix-all prayer that would make all the bad things go away.

I tried to meditate like my mother so that I could eventually find peace and kindness through the mantra, but my mind would not rest. It was always racing with a million thoughts. Today, I thought about the impending boredom long before I even had time to be bored. I thought about my brothers and what they must be doing while I was with Mother. I thought about my father, who had come with us to the temple today even though he had never come to prayers with us before. My father always did his prayers and visits to the monastery alone. The three of us had walked together, which never happened unless we were attending a funeral. A visit to the monastery for prayer just was not the kind of thing we did as a family. It was something I did to keep my mother happy.

"Om mani padme hum." My mother and I chanted again in unison. I kept my eyes mostly closed, as if I were trying to reach deep meditation, but I could still see a little bit through my eyelashes. Behind me, I could hear footsteps approaching. I could hear my father talking to someone. Even though he whispered, my father's voice boomed across the sacred hall of the monastery.

My mother said her last chant and gently turned toward me, then glanced to see my father with one of the main teachers in our village. I looked at them and they looked back at me with a slight grimace.

"This is Tenzin Lahkpa, our youngest," my father said, introducing me to the teacher. The monk nodded toward me in recognition of my presence.

I nodded back. It was odd. Even though I had been to the temple many times and had prayed with my mother there my entire life, I had never been formally introduced to one of the monks. They were a permanent fixture in our village, and even though I saw them almost every day walking around and praying, I had never really thought about them as human. They were teachers and holy priests. They existed on a different level of life than I did.

"When the time comes," the teacher said to my mother and father, "he will be welcomed here."

I almost fell over. I knew what those words meant.

9
AN OFFERING TO THE TEMPLE

When I left the monastery with my parents, I was in a dazed state of mind. I was not entirely sure of all that had just transpired, but I was certain that it was nothing I was going to enjoy.

My mother walked as if she were floating. Her body didn't wobble back and forth between her left stride and her right as it usually did. Instead, it was almost as if she were standing still on an invisible moving plank that was transporting her home. She was not smiling, but I could see a smile in her eyes.

And she was humming. She never hummed.

Without saying a word, my father stepped off to the left and went in a different direction. As usual, I had no clue where he was going, and on this occasion, I didn't much care. I had so many questions and couldn't get them out fast enough. I was sure that my father would not be as helpful as my mother in providing the answers to my questions.

"What was that about, Mother?" I asked her with great urgency.

She was in no hurry to answer my questions. Her eyes shifted toward me, and she smiled as she looked away again. She was happy with the answer to my question even before she delivered it.

"Why did we meet with the teacher just now?" I asked the next question before she had a chance to answer the first. "Mother, please. You can't do this to me. The suspense is killing me. Why did we meet with the monk today and what did he mean when he said I would be welcomed there?"

"Oh, my precious little boy," she replied as she kept walking. I was behind her when she spoke, but I could hear her smiling as she said the words.

"Mother, are you going to give me away to the monastery?" I asked her directly. "Stop, Mother. Please tell me! Are you going to give me away?"

"I cannot give what I do not have," she said.

"There we go with the Buddha talk," I protested against her indirect answer. It is typical in Buddhism to speak in the parables of Buddha instead of holding real conversations to establish yes or no answers. My mother was the master of it. You could ask her a million questions and she would answer each one of them at length but never actually give a real answer.

When I was a child, I would ask something like, "Mother, can I go out and play?" She would reply, "Only those with idle time spend it in play, but they will soon find that the next life will subtract their waste and add it to their burden. Idleness is only prolonged pain. You decide how long you would like to prolong it."

"Soooo…that means yes?" I would ask. "Yes or no—can I go outside and play with my friends?"

"True friends will not participate in folly, but guard you from it."

"Arrrgggggg." Why answer with a simple yes or no when complicated parables work just fine?

But today, we were not talking about going outside to play. We were talking about my life—my future.

We arrived home, and I was no closer to getting an answer out of her. My oldest brother burst through the door, but as soon as he saw me, he smiled. Our eyes met, and then he put his head down, moved across the room, and greeted my mother.

I followed him with my eyes. "What?" I asked him, but he only smiled and moved away, looking for something by the shelf bordering the bed. "What is so funny?" I demanded. "There isn't anything funny. Mother, what does he know?"

"Oh, you haven't told him, Mother?" my brother asked. His voice was polite and surprised, but he was still clearly mocking me.

"Told me what? What was she supposed to tell me?"

My brother simply shrugged his shoulders. "Ask Mother," he said as he walked out of the room.

I stood there and looked at my mother. She appeared angelic and calm as she sat down on the edge of our large family bed in the middle of the room. "I have been blessed with wonderful children, and they have all had good health," she said, deliberately leaving out the fact that one of my sisters had died before I was born. However, in Tibet, the odds of children surviving infancy were much lower than in other places in the world. Our hospitals are very primitive, and children and the elderly are the most vulnerable to diseases that are entirely curable with the proper treatment.

My mother continued, "The time has now come that I perform my duty for the gift of healthy children and make an offering to the temple."

I could feel the pressure build behind my eyes as they filled up with tears. My bottom lip began to quiver uncontrollably. I knew exactly what was happening—and it was my worst fear. I had seen many young boys my age brought by their parents to the temple to be given to live the life of a monk. Most of the time, it was a way for poor families to provide food, education, and a life of discipline for their child. But other times, it was a sacrifice required of devout families.

"From the moment you were born, I knew that you would be the one to honor our family and be a monk. I have dreamed about this day since you were very little. You were always so smart and kind. You were always so clever, and I knew that your purpose was to be a monk. I know that this is not easy for you to understand, but you were born to be a monk and lead our people into enlightenment. This is a special duty that not many people have been given. You must have done something very special in your former life to have such an honor."

I looked at my mother, not believing what she was saying to me. How could she just abandon me? Then she said the words that came crashing down on me like thunder: "Don't you want to honor me?"

There it was. There was the argument that ended all arguments. I had no way to reply. There was no defense. With that one sentence, my mother won the argument and shut me up. A son who becomes a monk can earn his mother's place in society. She will be respected and honored by everyone in her community. A mother who gives up her child to be a monk at the monastery is considered to be pious and holy.

If a son truly loves his mother and does not want her to experience Avici or one of the lower levels of hell, then he will ensure her peaceful afterlife by becoming a monk. If I resisted my mother and told her that I did not want to be a monk, then she would be shamed. Everyone would know that I did not truly love or respect her and that she was not worthy to go to heaven. For the rest of her life, she would be a woman to be pitied.

My mind raced back to the story of the disciple Moggallana, who fed the monks and clothed them and kept his mother from suffering in Avici. As a disciple of Buddha, he was able to earn his mother's place in heaven. I also recalled the many times my mother had told me the story of the beautiful Queen Maya, the mother of Buddha, who is the most respected woman in all of Buddhism. She is known in Tibet as Queen Gyutrulma, and there is no female holier than she. Queen Gyutrulma waited for years to become pregnant, and when she finally did, her pregnancy was proceeded by a prophetic dream. Tragically, she died only seven days after giving birth. Maya lived in heaven after her death and descended to earth on occasion to advise Buddha. The status of Buddha ensured her status in heaven.

The message was perfectly clear. If I loved my mother and wanted to see her go to heaven, then I would do my part and honor her by becoming a monk in the monastery.

10
MOVING DAY

It is impossible to talk about Tibetan culture without talking about the Tibetan Buddhist monks. They play a central role in the lives of the Tibetan people, and they guide every aspect of Tibetan life.

Not only do the monks care for the monasteries and help the people understand their religion and history, but they perform all of the marriages, funerals, and blessings of newborns. As I mentioned earlier, they even choose babies' names and determine their destiny.

The population of the Tibetan people is not very large compared to the rest of the population of China. In fact, the Han Chinese people make up the majority of the world population, but even with our few numbers, Tibetans make up the majority of Buddhist monks. The Tibetans dominate the Buddhist temples. There are tens of thousands of Tibetan monks who run the monasteries from Tibet to Beijing and everywhere in between. The provinces of Qinghai, Gansu, Sichuan, and Yunnan are each larger than a European country, and their Buddhist temples are run by Tibetans.

I was now going to be counted among their number.

On moving day, my father gently put his hand on my back as we walked toward the monastery. I do not remember him ever touching me in a gentle, loving manner like that before.

My mother was crying, but I could not convince myself that these were tears of sorrow because she did not indicate in any way that her tears were going to stop her from giving me over to the monks.

I shuffled my feet through the sand, taking my last steps of freedom.

After my mother had told me that I was going to be given over to the monastery, I began to look at everything in the village differently. When I saw the monks begging for food every day, I knew that this would be my future. When I saw children walking around in crimson robes, I realized I would wear nothing else than a maroon robe for the rest of my life. I no longer dreamed of a grand future shooting bows and arrows and winning every competition to bring my family honor. Now, I had nightmares of eternal, self-imposed poverty and horrible food.

I might never again know what it was like to sleep in a comfortable bed. I might never again have a warm, cooked meal to feast from. I was still only a teenager, but I was certain that I did not want to be celibate! All of the fanciful dreams I'd had of which girl I might marry were being thrown away.

"Om mani padme hum," my mother said aloud as she spun the first prayer wheel.

My father and I repeated after her and ran our hands across the prayer wheels, making them spin as we walked by.

I could hear other people chanting prayers and realized how few prayers I actually knew. I looked around and noticed a young boy who looked about half my age wearing a maroon robe. He was probably only seven or eight years old, but he prayed with confidence. I felt very ill-equipped.

Many monks join the monastery as young as five or six years old if they are approved by the *rinpoche*. A rinpoche is a senior lama who is the head of the monastery. He is generally regarded as the reincarnation of the monastery's founding lama. They are known for their ability to identify religious relics that have great meaning. As a symbol of their honorary position, they usually sit on a throne of cushions that is elevated above everyone else.

Monasteries do not like to take monks at too young of an age because they are not equipped to care for babies or toddlers. A young male monk must be ready and capable to serve, not to be served. Handicapped children have no place in a Buddhist monastery because they are not considered whole. If a child is born with deformities, deaf, blind, or paralyzed, they are not complete. They are further from the idea of enlightenment. Many monks teach that those who do not do well in their former lives can come back as a disabled person. Even though Buddha has disciples who could be considered to have physical deformities, they are not found in the Tibetan Buddhist monasteries. Additionally, those who are handicapped are not ideal for the jobs monks have to do while working in the temple and serving the senior monks.

One reason for sending young males off to serve in monasteries is that it provides the older teachers with a constant supply of free labor and allows a society to trim off the male population without the need for a war. A further advantage is that, in order to avoid problems with inheritance in a land dispute involving a younger son, the parents can dedicate the younger son to the temple.

Rinpoches have the power to recognize children who are reincarnate leaders that have obtained enlightenment in a former life. If the Rinpoche does not recognize a child as being a reincarnated monk, then parents who would like to bring that child to serve at the monastery must have them professionally trained first, and then the child must take a test. I did not require a test because my uncle was a well-known monk who served in Lhasa, the capital city of Tibet. It was actually not odd to have a monk in our family. In fact, it would have been odd if our family did *not* have a monk in it. Most families in Tibet have relatives who are serving in the local monastery.

Until I was told that I would be a monk, I had never realized how many monks were a part of my everyday life. And, as I mentioned earlier, I had never really thought of monks as being human like me. I knew that they were people who slept and ate and all of the things that people do, but I never really imagined the village monks to be someone's child or brother. It was not until that day that I saw the monks as real people who'd had to go through the same things I'd gone through while growing up. None of these monks had been born and raised in the monastery. As children, all of them had cried at night when they were hungry or scared. All of them had been spanked by their mothers for disobeying and doing things wrong. All of them had had to be nurtured by their parents from their infancy to grow to be strong to live in a monastery.

With these thoughts, the monks did not seem so mysterious to me anymore.

As we approached the door, one of the monks was there waiting for me. He nodded to my parents and motioned for me to walk with him. I turned to look at my parents one last time. They were no longer looking at me. My mother was gazing at the ground.

I wondered what they were thinking. Were they sad? Would they miss me? Would it be as if I were dead?

Without saying goodbye to them, I walked away. And just like that, I left home.

11
THE CRUCIBLE

I walked with the monk until a younger man came to meet us. "This is Tenzin Lahkpa," the monk said. "Get him situated."

"Yes, Teacher," said the young man. Then he moved his head in a forward direction, indicating that I was to follow him.

Everything was familiar and strange at the same time. I had grown up my entire life staring at the gods and goddesses on the walls of the monastery when we came to pray, but to know that I would not be leaving and going "home" made everything look different.

"I am Gyatso," the young man said while moving swiftly through the corridor, which was echoing with bells ringing and people chanting. "Do as I say at all times and do not ask questions. Do you understand?"

I nodded and tried to keep up.

"You will never need anything that we do not provide for you here. Everything that you need in life is here. If we do not have it, you do not need it. Understand? Forget the world outside of these walls. It is full of distractions and suffering. In here, you will suffer if you do not do exactly as I tell you. Understand?"

"Yes, I understand, but—"

I was going to ask where we were going, but Gyatso stopped abruptly. I didn't react fast enough and bumped into him.

"No. No. You don't need to talk. You—you listen! I do not need to hear your voice. You need to hear mine," he said, shoving me back and pointing in my face. "Understand?"

I nodded. As quickly as he had stopped, he started walking again, and we entered a room with five other young men.

"We have a new Pabbajja," Gyatso said, "and he needs a haircut." *Pabbajja* was a term I had never heard before. Many of the words that were being used that I didn't understand were Sanskrit—the primary language used in Hinduism. Several monks at the monastery studied and understood Sanskrit so that they could refer to ancient Buddhist texts. *Pabbajja* was the Sanskrit word for one who has left their home and renounced the world to live among fully ordained monks.

The five young men surrounded me. One of them had a stool, and before I knew what was going on, the stool had been swept to the back of my knees, causing me to fall into a sitting position.

Someone roughly grabbed my chin with one hand and forced my head back with the other. I felt as if my neck were about to snap off. I was looking up and could see nothing but six faces smashed together, looking down on me. "Time for a haircut," one of them said in a devious voice.

Then, using scissors in an almost saw-like fashion, they began to cut my hair. It was a mixture of pulling and cutting that was excruciating. I didn't fight it. I was ready for everything that they had for me. I was ready to accept my destiny. This was my path now. Cutting my hair was just the first step to renouncing the material world and embracing a journey of discovery.

I was scared and in pain, but this was eclipsed by a new excitement— knowing that I was becoming my own man and was no longer a child. This was the beginning of my training, which would eventually lead to honor. I would be on probation and would fail if I did not learn as quickly as possible. Failure was not really an option for me. I would humiliate my family and disgrace my entire village if I failed. I was determined to succeed and was ready to absorb everything I could and to learn as much as they would teach me.

I silently prayed to Buddha to give me strength. I prayed for his example to give me inspiration, wisdom, and power. I went into a state of intense meditation, imagining the good that these six young men were doing for me instead of focusing on the pain they were causing me.

All of my mother's words came rushing back to me, flooding my thoughts, including her teachings about ridding myself of all worldly desires. I tried to make myself calm down and show the other monks that I had no fear, that they did not intimidate me and could not hurt me.

"I am going to do this," I said to myself. "Even if it kills me, I am going to do this."

12
MY DAILY BREAD

My first year in the monastery was not an easy one, but it got easier every day. I spent the first month crying myself to sleep every night. I missed being in the large bed with all of my family. I longed for the morning smells of breakfast being cooked by my mother.

Before I came to the temple, I didn't have a clue about what monks actually did all day. In my mind, monks spent their time walking around cold, dusty hallways chanting, and taking breaks to pray, meditate, and beg for food. I had heard about monks who meditated for weeks at a time without stopping for food or water. To me, that sounded like nothing more than an extended nap that eventually led to waking up with a hungry stomach and a serious need for a good stretch.

However, what I hadn't realized was how much monks had to work! Every minute of every hour was planned for us. I worked harder in my first year as a monk than I had done at any other time in my life. I was always busy cleaning, studying, or running from one part of the monastery to the other to catch up after falling behind. There was never any leisure time. Ever. My former enjoyment of Buddhist festivals was long gone because festivals were our busiest times.

The teachers were extremely strict and demanding, and they loved making us work hard. It was no wonder they had so much time to meditate. They had all of the students to take care of them. I was either helping the teachers, cleaning up for the teachers, washing the dirty dishes or clothing of the teachers, pouring tea for the teachers, preparing the cushions for the teachers to sit on, or arranging the teaching materials for the teachers. And that was 24-7 every day, with no vacation days. If the teachers needed something at two in the morning, then they could (and did) send for us to come and assist them.

If there wasn't anything extra to do, then every day basically looked like this:

0600: Wake up (0500 on special holidays)

0630: Go to kitchen to make breakfast for teachers

0730: Eat breakfast—while simultaneously serving a teacher

0830: Clean up

1000: Study time

1100: Prayer time

1200: Lunch

1400: Meditation time

1600: Study time

1800: Prepare dinner

1900: Eat dinner—while simultaneously serving a teacher

1930: Clean up

2030: Prayer time (festivals included prayer with villagers until midnight)

Not only was the work harder than when I had worked on the family farm, but I was never paid for my labor. Those who think they are escaping poverty or hard work by becoming a monk are sorely mistaken. There were so many things that I had been hoping to learn during my first year, but I spent most of my time trying to catch my breath. Yet, even though I was so busy, I felt that I had purpose. I hadn't seen any specific sign of my purpose, but I had the hope of discovering it.

I had never spent much time in school, so there were many things I did not know. I was intrigued with each session given by a teacher. I was fascinated with the stories and the writings of Buddha.

Gyatso was also a wealth of information. I'd never had any friends who were as smart as he was. He knew how to speak three forms of Tibetan—Kamda, Amdo, and Central Tibetan. He could also read Sanskrit and Chinese, and he was studying English.

Gyatso had lived at the monastery since he was only seven years old. He was not kind and loving like my mother, but I felt safe around him. He was tough yet fair. If I would fall behind or do something wrong, he would slap me, punch me, or kick me. As odd as it is to say, I believe this was all done with love. It was an honor to serve together with him. He was a dedicated monk and did not hold anything back in his search for truth.

I thought that I had always lived a simple life because my family was so poor, but I learned that things at the temple were much simpler. I was taught to follow the example of Buddha in everything. Part of this was to throw away all of my clothing, after which I received a simple robe to wear. I kept my head shaved, and I ate only small portions of whatever I was given, with no regard for taste.

I had only one silver bowl, which was given to me to eat out of every day. It was the only thing I really owned and went everywhere with me. When I was given the bowl, I was told that this was the only bowl I would ever use to eat from for the rest of my life.

I disciplined my mind to neither like nor dislike food. I heard other young boys who were training at the monastery talk about the foods they missed the most from home, and I felt the same way at first, but then I realized how much pain that was causing me. I had to let go of all attachments related to this earthly world in order to achieve enlightenment.

One day, during one of the lectures, we had a visiting monk who taught us about the constant war between the mind and the body. Our earthly body maintains thirsts, desires, and longings that go beyond what we need for survival. After we have what we need to survive, our body craves even more, and when we feed these thirsts and desires, our body still craves more. It is a constant cycle that can occupy every thought of our mind and never cease. It spins around and around like the prayer wheel because our bodies are greedy. Our greed is insatiable and self-destructive.

"Greed is the number one roadblock to enlightenment," the monk said. "Even the simple, sensual flavors on our taste buds can control our thoughts and occupy us until the day we die. Those who give in to the flavors of food can never obtain true enlightenment because they are controlled by the lust of their stomachs. Their minds are fully occupied by food, and when their day of death finds them, they will have nothing to account for all of their days on earth except for the time they spent searching for food."

His teaching was truly fascinating. He made the words of Buddha come alive to me. This made me think about all of the time that I had spent missing my mother's cooking and how I'd wished that I could go beg for food by my old house so that my mother could come out and place some of my favorite dishes in my bowl. My mouth watered at the thought of it.

"If we spend every day searching for the food that we desire, this makes us no different from the animals that are many steps away from enlightenment. Dogs spend all of their waking moments looking for food. They are slaves to their stomachs. So when we die and our reincarnation is assigned, why would it not be a blessing for us to come back as a dog? Today, we are men and are closer to enlightenment than any other being on earth. Being a man is a gift. If we waste the gift on searching for food instead of truth, then why do we deserve our gift?"

His words shot through me and convicted me of my own desires. I didn't want to come back as a dog. I didn't want to waste the opportunity that had been given to me.

13
THE PRAYER FLAGS

"Tenzin, have you found peace today?" Teacher Tashi Lama asked as we sat down together for the day's reading.

"Yes, Teacher," I replied.

It was true. I had found peace. I was much calmer than I had ever remembered being. I was not anxious about anything. Like a fish in a bowl, all I knew in life were the surroundings of the walls that confined me to my fishbowl and the view of the sky when I looked up. Everything that I needed to know could be found in my own bowl.

I was also much happier at the monastery than I had ever been. When I was working in the fields and herding our animals, I was always dreaming of when my work would be over. I had to worry about the crops getting enough water. I had to worry about the yaks being taken by a neighboring village. I was beginning to really understand what Buddha's teachings were all about.

There were ninety-seven monks in our monastery and thirty-one of them were teachers. It is required for every new monk to have a teacher who takes them as one of their disciples to train for life, and Teacher Tashi Lama had taken me under his tutelage. Young monks learn from a master lama. They spend all day, every day, with their lama, who invests his energy in the lives of his disciples. It is a very close relationship and keeps the teaching as near to the source as possible. The lama eats, sleeps, and lives life with his disciples, and through this relationship, the trainees learn things over time that they would never learn from a book.

I had been assigned to Tashi Lama immediately because he had noticed I have a mark on my right hand. He said that it was a sign from a past life that he had taught me previously. "We all carry signs that trace us back to our past lives," he told me. "If we only know what we are looking for, our bodies can tell us a story of who we really are and what we are destined to be. It is possible to communicate with the spirits all around us if we will only listen. The spirits can tell us everything we need to know about ourselves. Our position in life has already been determined, and we carry marks on our bodies to point us to the truth."

In Tibet, when a child is born, their body is checked for signs, moles, or birthmarks. Simple things—like having big ears similar to Buddha's—are considered to be a sign of wisdom. There were many mysteries that I was slowly starting to unravel, but it was not easy. There were so many things to know and so many sources to learn them from.

Though many Buddhist monks study one form of Buddhism or another, Tibetan monks study all forms of Buddhism. Tibetan Buddhism is a mix of Theravada, Mahayana, Vajrayana, Hinduism, and the ancient animistic Tibetan religion of Bön.

"This is one of our ancient secrets," Tashi Lama told me, referring to the ancient religion of the Tibetan people that goes back thousands of years. "Our belief is grounded in the earth and cannot be given a name. It is the secret source of all that is real. It is our ability to communicate with both gods and demons as well as with the dead and living that gives us power."

When Tashi Lama said this, I was not certain if he was teaching, meditating, or in some sort of state between the two. "See our prayer wheels?" he asked me. I nodded my head once. "Where else do you see them but among our people? Look to the mountains. What do you see on our mountains that you do not see on any other mountains?"

I didn't know how to answer. I had never been to any other location and had never seen any mountains other than those in Tibet.

"*Prayer flags!*" his voice snapped through the air.

Prayer flags are the colorful, rectangular pieces of cloth that flap in the wind from every high point in Tibet. They often dangle from a single string like laundry hanging out to dry.

"My son, we are the highest place in the world. No other place on earth is as high as we are. This is not by mistake. Our early masters brought us here to possess the peaks." He leaned in, coming out of his meditative state and putting his finger in the air for dramatic effect. "In any battle, the highest peak is the most prized possession. High ground is the terrain that has been recognized for thousands of years as the most valuable position during battle. Soldiers fighting uphill will tire more quickly, while those repelling them can fight going downhill and move faster with less energy. At the moment, the earthly prize of the high ground belongs to the Tibetan spirits, and any intruder is literally fighting an uphill battle. When military units conquer the high land, the first thing they do is to plant a flag so that everyone around them can see who the victor is. Those who are winning are energized and those who are losing look up and see the flag and are demoralized.

"Watch the flags. They never sleep. They never rest. They forever whip in the wind as they are stirred by the moving of the spirits of the secret world. The spirits pass over the mountains and through the flags like drag-ons slithering to and fro over the ridgelines of the mountains."

The prayer flags come in five colors—yellow, green, red, white, and blue—that represent the five elements: earth, water, fire, air, and sky or darkness. I had been taught from an early age to carry the prayer flags to the top of the mountains where they would signal to those in the valley that the spirits never sleep and forever emit spiritual vibrations. Suddenly, the flags I had grown up seeing everywhere made more sense.

"Shhheeeeee," said Tashi Lama, making a sound like a rushing wind. "The ancient spirits cry out and we must listen."

Right as he said that, I felt a quick breeze brush over my skin. The hair on my arms stood straight up.

"There is no good and evil. We must wipe our minds of such dualism because it does not exist. There is only one single power that controls us all, and it is neither good nor evil."

Tashi Lama was actually more than a lama. He was our local shaman for the monastery. A shaman is a spiritual leader who has access to the spiritual world and can communicate with the dead, cast spells, see the future, interpret dreams, and create secret potions for sickness or wealth. Shamans were in bigger demand in my home village because of their ability to move into the spirit world and control the actions of demons that would bring harm.

"Close your eyes, my son," Tashi Lama said. He lifted up both of his hands, with his palms facing his face. "The spirits are here. Invite them into your soul. Let them flood your thoughts and control your mind. Let the spirits guide you and teach you. Let them live in you and through you. They know the path and will lead you to enlightenment."

As Tashi Lama chanted, I could feel the power of his prayers in the room. The air was moving. Even the ground under me seemed to be unsta-ble. "Do not be afraid. You will not die, because there is no death, only transition. In the grand time of the universe, we change bodies, shape, size, sex, and species, but we never die. We do not need to fear death. We only need to fear the lingering pain of hanging on to one form of life longer than we should."

I took both of my hands out of my lap and placed them on the ground beside me. I was getting dizzy, and I needed stabilization. I opened my eyes to see that Tashi Lama was in complete control of everything. His words flowed out with seeming command of all the elements in the room. He was as close to communicating with the spirit world as anyone or anything I had ever met. I had seen this kind of thing before with my mother and father when they would take me to the monastery to pray for guidance or protection, but I had always thought it was kind of fake.

But this was real. I could feel it. I was witnessing its power.

I was glad that Tashi Lama was on my side. I was happy to be his disciple. He had the power in his prayers to summon the demons and gods—but that was not the only reason I was glad I was his disciple. It was because there were much darker things happening at night in the monastery with other lamas that I did not have to experience. Things I did not want to imagine.

14
DARK SECRETS

Lying on my flat mat, which was spread out on the floor next to the mats of the other students, I could hear the sounds of the night. The long, busy days at the monastery made me look forward to evening time when I could finally rest. During the periods of the day when we were supposed to be praying or studying, I would fight to stay awake. So, normally, at night, I would fall into a deep sleep almost as fast as I could roll out my mat. However, on some nights, like tonight, eerie sounds echoing through the still night air of the monastery shook me from my sleep. The sounds were not loud, but they were out of place. They seemed to be faint cries coming from another part of the temple.

I had not known where they were coming from and hadn't dared to get up to find out. I had thought they were possibly the cries of spirits or demons that had come to haunt us, but now I knew they were cries of pain coming from one of the younger boys. He was crying for the same reason other little boys had cried before him. It was because he was going through a physically and emotionally painful experience.

I had learned about the night cries earlier that day. Several of us monks-in-training had gone down to a nearby stream to bathe and swim. One of the boys whom I knew well and who was much younger than I took off his robe. I was shocked when I noticed marks across his back that looked like scars from being whipped by a leather strap.

"What happened to him?" I asked in general.

Gyatso looked in the direction where I was looking to see who I was referring to. Then, he looked at me and said, "Oh, that is Gantdo Lama."

I didn't need to ask another question. I knew exactly what had happened. Gyatso was not saying that the boy's name was Gantdo Lama; he was saying that what had happened to him had been done by Gantdo Lama.

Gantdo Lama was one of the meanest and most violent monks in the monastery. Everyone was afraid of him. He beat his disciples on a regular basis, and he was always yelling and screaming at others. One time, he damaged part of an altar when he got into a fight with one of the worshippers who had come into the monastery, accidentally gotten in his way, and not shown him the proper respect.

"Poor guy," Gyatso said about the boy. "He tried to escape but was caught and beaten by Gantdo Lama."

"Why did he try to escape?" I asked.

"Shhhhh…keep it down," Gyatso said as he looked around to see if anyone else was listening. "You don't know?"

I shook my head no.

"You really do not know?" he asked again in a lower but more incredulous voice. "Because he is Gantdo's new dakini."

A *dakini* is often the term for someone who is used for sexual pleasure by Tibetan lamas. I had heard my brothers use the word before, but I hadn't heard many people use it since I had been living at the temple.

"You know, you should count yourself lucky that you have never had to deal with Gantdo Lama. That guy turns all of his disciples into dakinis during their first year of service."

Many of the lamas at our temple had secret wives that they would sneak out to meet, while others had dakinis, but I had never imagined they would use the boy monks for this. We both looked over again at the wounds on the back of the young boy. They were hard to look at. "Man, these lamas," Gyatso said. "They think they can do whatever they want and get away with it. They walk around like they are so holy and enlightened, but so many of them are child rapists."

Gyatso was not wrong. The lamas are powerful individuals, and their power goes largely unchecked because they answer to no one outside of ecclesiastical authority. The Tibetan temples deal with sexual fantasies as they see fit and answer to no one on the outside about their practices.

"The teachings here really blur the lines, you know? I mean, the first thing that they do is tell you that there is no such thing as good and evil. They remove the boundaries between what you think is good and what you think is bad. After a while, everything is relative. From day one, we are taught that pain is the result of desire, and enlightenment is giving yourself over to where boundaries no longer exist. Oh yeah, they love that. That way, when you feel the pain of them raping you, it is your problem—not theirs!"

I couldn't tell because of the sunlight glistening on the water, but it almost looked as if tears were welling up in Gyatso's eyes. I stayed silent. I was listening, but I waded into the water and slowly swished it a little with my hands. I thought that by pretending not to fully notice his tears and painful words, it might lessen his pain.

"If a victim is in pain, it is the result of their lack of desire to serve," he continued. "A monk must serve his master." Gyatso's words were angry. There was nothing I could say or do to help him, so I continued to pretend not to be too invested.

"My parents never would have left me here if they had known that this was going on," he said. "I should never have taken the oath of that stupid samaya!"

I froze. *Samaya* is the most sacred bond between a disciple and teacher and can never be broken. When I entered into the agreement with Tashi Lama, it was a sacred moment in which I promised to give him my speech, mind, and body. Once you enter into the samaya, you can never leave unless you want to experience eternal torment.

There are fourteen ways that the samaya can be broken and all of them are very serious. According to the teachings of Tibetan Buddhism, a few of the ways to break the samaya are disrespecting your master, disobeying the words of the Buddhas, or criticizing the teachings of the Buddhas. The worst is revealing the secrets of Buddhism to those who are unworthy. But not taking the secret oath of the samaya was blasphemous, and breaking the oath would earn a monk the most torturous part of hell. In Tibetan Buddhism, there are eighteen different levels of hell. Level eighteen is the most painful and excruciating—and it is reserved for people who break the samaya.

That night, as I lay on my mat and heard the cries of the young boy, I could not help but think about Gyatso's words. Surely his parents would never have brought him to the temple to live the life of a monk if they had known what happened to many of the young boys after dark. I am certain that my parents did not know. The last thing we thought anyone would see at the monastery was sex. It never crossed our minds.

According to the teachings of Tashi Lama, I was not to engage in any sexual activities. This was one of the first teachings I received, and it was pounded into my head over and over again. Having sex of any kind was a serious monastic transgression that was ranked among theft, murder, and lying. Even masturbation was considered to be an offense that would get a monk kicked out of the monastery.

The prohibition had seemed pretty clear to me at the time, but it was not so clear anymore. The very thing that I had been told was wrong was being practiced by one of the senior teachers, and there was nothing I could do about it. Tashi Lama's teachings were not as insightful as they had been when I first arrived—they were getting more and more predictable—but at least he wasn't abusive.

Lying there in the night and listening to the cries of Gantdo's disciple, I realized that this was one of the secrets that I would never be able to share with those outside of the temple. Sharing the secrets was a damning offense that would send me to level eighteen of hell.

The longer I lived at the temple, the more secrets I would learn, but these secrets did not come with real knowledge. To obtain knowledge, I would someday have to seek another teacher.

15
FIRST PUBLIC DEBATE

One by one, the monks from our monastery walked into the village courtyard. Many of the local villagers followed us into the entrance.

"How did I get myself into this?" I thought.

The village square was now full of crimson robes and bald heads. Everyone sat in a neat formation facing the middle, except for a monk known as Somo—and me. Together, we waited for Tashi Lama.

It was debate day, and Somo and I were the main attraction. Our job was to debate for two to three hours in front of the entire village. Everyone was ready to watch two philosophical giants go at it, but I was fearfully unprepared.

Most likely, my parents and other family members had come out to see my first debate as a monk-in-training and were standing somewhere in the crowd, but I was not ready for this. I was about to shame my parents. That is how shame often works in our culture; it mostly concerns something you can or cannot do, and it is often based on things that are out of your control. Shame usually plagues the innocent.

It was true that debates were nothing new to me. Our monastery had debates almost every day. We debated each other in order to keep our minds sharp and build on the information we had learned. Yet outside of these regular debates, several times a year, our monastery performed public debates on different subjects as they pertained to our faith, and the village crowd got to decide the winner.

Somo was well-known as one of the best debaters in our monastery. He was masterful and commanded respect when he spoke. Even the lamas failed to subdue his intellectual arguments. According to the older lamas, he was the reincarnation of a great lama.

"I do not think that public debating is for me," I had told Tashi Lama the day before.

"You have been chosen. Your name was drawn from the lots," he said matter-of-factly. "You have fear," he said, confidently identifying why I did not want to debate.

Of course I had fears! There were several levels of debate that we test for, and Somo was at one of the highest levels. I was still at the beginning level. It was going to be a bloodbath.

"Don't try to look for your mistakes when you debate. Mistakes give birth to the blindness to your own folly. Look for seeds in the questions and give birth to truth through those seeds that Somo hands you. Fear will pull you to two paths—one is to freeze and the other is to panic. Look for the middle path between freezing and panic. There you will find your footing."

Since I had arrived at the monastery, I had been afraid of so many things. I had been fearful of joining the monastery. I had been fearful of the teachers and tests. I had been fearful of not being able to fit in. Every day gave me a different reason to be fearful. Tomorrow was little more than a promise of new fears. And the thought of standing out there in front of all the people who had come to watch me debate was a kind of fear I had never felt before.

I wondered if I would ever get used to the fear. Would I eventually build up a callous resistance to it, or would I build up a deficit of fear so large that all my other feelings would be attached to it?

Still, being fearful had not been all bad. Fear had given me a heightened feeling of self-awareness. Those demons on my shoulder had also been my guardians. The words they whispered only brought fear because their wisdom exposed my vulnerable ignorance. My fear of debating others had greatly contributed to my education—I had dived into my studies to prepare my defensive walls as best I could. In rare moments, I'd had glimpses of inspiration, but none more inspiring than the devil of fear....

The day before had been long, and I hadn't gotten any sleep during the night. My body had been tired, but my mind would not rest. Nothing wakes you up in the middle of the night like a nice warm plate of remorse. I knew that there were so many things I hadn't studied properly for the debate. I had lain in bed all night thinking of all the things I didn't know.

Now, standing in front of the crowd, in the sun, I was feeling nauseous from my lack of sleep. Somo was going to eat me up and spit me out.

Tashi Lama led me to the middle of the courtyard and motioned with his hand for me sit on the ground. I was the defender. My job was to verify, accept, and defend a statement of truth. Somo would try hard to get me to contradict myself. If I failed, it would be clear that I had more learning to do. But if I failed miserably, then my place at the monastery would be questioned. An overwhelmingly miserable performance would point to the fact that I did not belong among the monks and lamas seeking truth.

"Om a ra pa ca na dhih." The words of the mantra were prayed in a loud, high-pitched tone as an appeal to the Buddha of wisdom to start the debate.

Then Somo stood up, carefully placed his feet shoulder-width apart, and towered over me. He tipped his head in a bowing motion and then leaned down to make perfect eye contact. "With a mind free from greed and unfriendliness, incorruptible and purified, the noble disciple is already, during this lifetime, assured of four things: First, if there is a heaven, and if there is a cause and effect of good and bad actions, then it may be that, after death, I shall be reborn in heaven." He clapped loudly to dispel the demons of confusion and raised his left hand to heaven as if to draw my spirit closer to it.

I sat for a moment, then softly said, "I accept." How could I not accept? Somo was quoting the most famous teaching of Buddhist scripture.

"And if there is no heaven, no reward and no punishment of good and bad actions, then I live, at least here in this world, a happy life, free from hate and unfriendliness. But if there is karma for both bad and good, then bad things will happen to bad people and good things will happen to good people. How can I, doing no bad things, meet with a bad karma fate? I am even more consoled if karma does not exist and we, in fact, live in a world where bad things do not happen to bad people either." Somo again ended with a thunderous clap that was meant to send the demons of confusion away.

"I accept." My only defense from the sitting position was to oppose Somo with scripture and logic, but again, he was quoting directly from our basic Buddhist teachings, which spring from the Four Noble Truths. These Four Noble Truths are the essence of what it means to be Buddhist. They are the foundational teachings on which all else is built:

1. *Suffering exists.*
2. *Suffering arises from desire.*
3. *Suffering ceases when desire ceases.*
4. *Freedom from suffering is possible by practicing the Eightfold Path.*

The Four Noble Truths are observable truths rather than dogmatic beliefs that are accepted by faith. They can be defended by both the mind and the heart, and they were great to bring up at a debate because they are so logical. Unlike many of the other aspects of Tibetan Buddhism, which delve into spirits, demons, creation stories, and the like, the Four Nobel Truths can be logically explained and defended.

I had been afraid that Somo would start to argue points about the existence of gods or goddesses, but he did not. He stayed pretty basic. I started to realize that I didn't need to have any big concerns about his challenges in a public debate. Maybe it was because someone had told him not to discuss certain things. Maybe it was because, as monks, it was our duty to protect "normal" people from things that we knew they could not understand. Whatever the reasons, I was happy about it.

As the debate continued, I became more confident. It got to the point where I felt like I was the judge and jury of what was right and wrong—not the crowd. It was as if Somo's performance was for me instead of for a pursuit of truth. Somo made statements and attempted to prove them to *my* satisfaction.

I could not see my parents, but I knew that they were there watching. I knew that they were proud to see their friends and neighbors admiring their son. It was a feeling of power that I had never felt before.

16
MOTHERLY GUIDANCE

"Did you hear the news?" my mother asked. I hadn't seen her in almost a year. She often came to the temple, but I was always engaged in prayer, study, or work during the times she usually visited.

Everything in me wanted to hug her and tell her all that had been happening, but I was forbidden to touch her. Women in general were considered to be a distraction, and the energy from my mother, the one who had given me life, might take away from my desire to detach myself from the world. I had to stand at a distance from her and engage her only in passing.

I didn't acknowledge that she had asked me a question, but it didn't stop her from continuing to share the news with me. "Your oldest brother is getting married," she said in a hurried whisper, knowing that the time was short. "I just thought you should know the good news from me."

The information came as a jolt to my system. Of course, I knew that all of my brothers would one day get married. That was natural. However, it was a reminder of what I would never have.

Every day, women came to the temple to pray. Some of them were young and some of them were old. Most of them were married, but a number of them were not. They moved more gracefully than the men, and I could smell their fragrance above the incense burning at the altar. I had never noticed the scent of a woman as being anything different from that of a man until I was forced to live with a group of guys. My brother would never have to know what it was like to live without that scent.

"Also, have you heard anything about your uncle in Lhasa?" Just like that, my mother had quickly moved on to the next subject. She was always up-to-date with the gossip. Our village did not have a newspaper because it did not need one. My mother always knew what was happening and who was involved. "He is really high up, you know? He could pull some strings for you. You should connect with him. He would love to hear from you."

My mother was referring to her brother, who served as a monk in Lhasa. He was a high-ranking lama and was well-known among the Tibetan people for his teachings. He was one of the most famous Tibetan lamas from our hometown and was the pride of our family. My mother never let people forget it!

"Go and see him. It is your duty to the family," she said. And with that, she turned and left.

I stood there realizing that my road to enlightenment had quite possibly already been paved by my mother. Everything that I needed to know had come either directly or indirectly from her. Even my being a disciple of Tashi Lama, who had taught me so much, had come about as a result of my mother's efforts. She had been involved from the beginning to help select who would be my teacher. Tashi Lama might think that he had chosen me to be his disciple, but it was more likely that my mother had chosen him.

My mother knew that I had never been a great student, but that didn't matter because no book could be as powerful as spending every day with Tashi Lama and listening to his teachings. Personal apprenticeship, not book learning, is the essence of what Buddhism is all about. So, first I learned from my mother and father and then I learned from my master.

It was a pattern established by Buddha himself. He had not written books and forced students to study from them. He had passed along his teachings through other people. For about forty-five years after Buddha discovered enlightenment, he traveled around India and taught diverse groups of disciples. Even though both Buddha and his disciples were very well-educated and literate, nothing that Buddha said was ever written down during his lifetime. Instead, his disciples were chosen to memorize the basic tenets of each teaching and share what they learned with others. That is how Buddhism grew. It was not until later that those teachings were written down.

Tibetans believe that Buddha did not write anything down because discipleship was the most powerful and intimate way to obtain enlightenment.

Enlightenment is spiritual, not academic. The things that need to be understood can't be passed down in a sterile environment.

I followed the Galugpa form of Tibetan Buddhism, which was founded by a great Amdo Tibetan teacher who passed down his teachings through discipleship. Several hundred years ago, there were various ideas about Buddhism coming from India, so my village held a formal debate competition among the monks, and the elders of the village determined a winner. The winner became the teacher and the losers had to either leave the village or become the disciples of the winner. Our village then selected young boys to study under the winner of the debate, and this was the beginning of Galugpa Tibetan Buddhism.

Even though the main emphasis is on discipleship, that does not mean we abandoned or dishonored the ancient writings of wisdom. There were so many writings that we honored and studied every day, but even the writings were based on the oral traditions passed down by the disciples of Buddha.

The suggestion of visiting my uncle in Lhasa lingered in my mind for a while after my mother left. If I wanted to understand more and obtain enlightenment, then finding the best lama teachers should be my priority. Although Tashi Lama was an amazing teacher, there was only so much enlightenment he would be able to give me from his limited exposure.

Tashi Lama had never been to Lhasa, the capital of Tibetan Buddhism. He had never studied from one of the great monks. He had barely been out of our small mountain village. Tashi Lama was wise, but was he knowledgeable? There is a difference. Wisdom can apply to insight, while knowledge is learned and experienced.

I began to pace and pray, chanting the mantras of power to lead and guide me. I prayed for wisdom from the Buddha and the Dalai Lama. I rubbed my fingers over the *trengwa*, the prayer beads that hung from my hand, to help me recite my prayers in order. I thought of my mother and her guidance.

I prayed the mantra of "om tare tuttare ture soha," for wisdom from the mother of all Buddhas, the Green Dolma. The Green Dolma is a goddess from Lhasa who was born from a tear when it hit the ground on Red Hill. I prayed to her because I knew that she could assist me in finding the knowledge of enlightenment.

I repeated the Tara Mantra offered up to the Green Dolma as I ran my fingers over a smooth, round, wooden bead of my trengwa. The Tara Mantra is the prayer that is prayed when one is hoping to see one's needs met or is seeking special guidance. Each bead helped to remind me of the number of times I had repeated the mantra. As I recited the mantra, I could see the face of my mother on the face of the Green Dolma, telling me to go to Lhasa.

I again chanted, "Om tare tuttare ture soha." The purpose of saying it over and over again was to allow the mantra to join in the echo of eternity to please the divine. It etched the words and the meaning into your mind. Each word had meaning, and I meditated on the meaning as the symbols vibrated through the roof of my mouth.

The sound *om* is found in most chanting and mantras. It is holy and is the sound of spiritual silence in our spirit. By starting off a mantra with "om," I was preparing my spiritual being to leave the physical world.

The next word is *tare* or "Tara"—Dolma, the mother of Buddha whom I was praying to.

After that is *tuttare ture*, which roughly translates as "quick delivery of the spiritual path that I am seeking."

At the very end is *soha*, which is a proclamation signifying that the goddess of Dolma can be found in me.

I repeated the Tara Mantra over and over again, hoping to gain insight into my future. I desperately needed the mother of all Buddhas to help me.

The more I prayed, the more I felt strongly that I should travel to Lhasa.

17
THE TIBETAN PRACTICE OF SPIRITUAL SUICIDE

Whack!

I was hit on the top of the head with a long, one-inch-thick, wooden rod. "Start over," Tashi Lama said. "These are holy scriptures. You can't just say the words as you like."

I wanted to reach up and rub my head to make the throbbing pain go away, but I knew that it would be shameful to react to it.

It was a common experience for me to be hit on the head, back, chest, or arms when taught by Tashi Lama. He always carried a wooden stick with him as he instructed me to read and recite holy scriptures.

I had never imagined how many texts there were to memorize. There were thousands of ancient Buddhist writings, and I was required to know them and memorize large portions of them. Today, I was reading from the Sutras. The Sutras are the holy scriptures of Buddhism that are regarded as the oral teachings of Buddha.

"It is important to read the scriptures aloud properly if you want to travel to Lhasa. To read them aloud puts us in touch with Buddha and his teachings. To read them aloud incorrectly leads others astray. The seeds of enlightenment cannot be planted with incorrect recitation, just like the seeds of a flower cannot be sown in the wrong soil."

Tashi Lama was in support of my idea to travel to Lhasa to see my uncle. However, he had insisted that I stay on to study for a couple of more years in order to be prepared.

"You must decide how you will live and how you will die. Once you die, it is impossible for you to change. If you are in darkness and read scripture with a virtuous heart, you will head toward the light. If you are in the light and read scripture with negative energy, you will head toward the darkness. Read again."

"In one whose persistence is aroused, a rapture not-of-the-flesh arises," I read in a monotone voice clashing with the voices around me. "When a rapture not-of-the-flesh arises in one whose persistence is aroused, then rapture as a factor for Awakening becomes aroused. He develops it, and for him it goes to the culmination of its development. For one who is enraptured, the body grows calm and the mind grows calm. When the body and mind of an enraptured monk grow calm, then serenity as a factor for Awakening becomes aroused. He develops it, and for him it goes to the culmination of its development."

I was reading from a prose known as "The Seven Factors of Enlightenment."

"What is the single greatest obstacle to enlightenment?" Tashi Lama asked.

I froze at his question. "There are five hindrances to enlightenment: greed, ill-will, doubt, worry—"

Tashi Lama cut me off before I mentioned laziness, or sloth. "I do not want you to quote me something that you have read. What have you learned from me? What have you learned from yourself? What do all five of those hindrances have in common?"

I sat silent, staring at the text in front of me. I desperately did not want to get hit again by the stick.

"You. You are the problem. Ill-will, laziness, sloth, worry, and doubt are all inside of you. These are not outside factors that have any influence on you; they are you having influence on outside factors. You have the power, and you are the hindrance. If you are to achieve understanding, you must be able to recognize the obstacles, even if the obstacle is you. Beyond recognizing the problem, you must be ready to remove the problem—even if the problem is you."

"How do I remove myself?" I asked.

"You must kill yourself."

His answer shocked me.

"You must die to yourself and those things inside of you that connect you to this world. There is a daily battle inside of you that you need to have cut out and removed. There are demons that attach themselves to your spirit and war inside of you that create greed, laziness, and fear—the obstacles that keep you from obtaining enlightenment."

"How do I do this?" I asked.

"By the Tibetan Rite of Chod."

The Rite of Chod. I had learned about this before. It was a gruesome visualization of dying to yourself by chopping yourself into pieces and giving your body over as a dead sacrifice. There was a burial place in the mountains that monks liked to journey to at night, when the demons were the most active, and lie down on the ash heaps where bodies are burned. This was a way to act out a sacrifice of self.

"Your mind," Tashi Lama said as he poked himself in the head with his index finger so hard that I could hear it. In his other hand, he held a small *damaru*, which is a two-sided drum used for death ceremonies. "Your mind is a vehicle for demons that attach themselves to you. They do not want temples and shrines made of wood and brick. They want to live in you. You are their temple. These demons bind you to form. They teach you to overemphasize your attachments to this world."

He turned the damaru from side to side so that the leather strap swung a small bead that struck the leather face of each side of the drum.

"You need only to visualize the demons feasting on your body. Picture yourself with your inner eye—decapitated, with the vultures of the underworld devouring you piece by piece. Do not resist them. You have nothing to resist because you do not exist. Give yourself over to them, because you are no longer you. You are dead. Your ego is crucified. Once they consume the pieces that you offer, they will have nothing more to eat and will move on and your spirit will be free from attachments.

"The only demon that keeps you from obtaining ultimate awareness is the demon of self. It is the demon that all the other demons attach to. Once you slay the demon of self, the others will have to go elsewhere to survive. Once you remove self, there is nothing else that can bring you pain."

His words were making sense to me. When I thought about all the times my mother or brothers said something that hurt me, I realized that they had only hurt my ego—my self-image. My pain came from my ego. The "me" or the "I" in me wanted to be loved, and if my ego didn't feel loved, then I felt pain.

My pain did not really exist at all. Without my ego, I would not have felt the pain. My wounds, which were created by what others did or said to me, were all self-inflicted. They were not real. They were my own creations.

"How can you be offended if you do not exist to be offended? Does a tree care if you do not love it? Does the wind stop blowing if you hurt its feelings? Is the mountain not as high if you despise it? Like the tree, wind, and mountain, we must empty ourselves and detach from the demon of self."

Tashi Lama's words were swirling around in my head, and their meaning was growing. They were building blocks to newer, more complex ideas.

"In this Chod is power—real spiritual power that belongs to the gods. I am not just talking about obtaining understanding. I am talking about the ability to defy the laws of nature, cure disease, and place curses on your enemies."

Place curses on my enemies?

This was a power I had not previously touched on in my studies. I was interested in learning more. Little did I know that I would learn the *hard way* regarding Tashi Lama's curses on his enemies.

Labrang Lamasery temple.

Tibetan Buddhists at prayer.

The Temple of Mysteries (Jokhang Temple), Lhasa, Tibet.

Potala Palace, Lhasa.

Lhamo La-tso (Lhamo Latso), Tibet.

Himalayan trekking.

Prayer flags in the Himalayas.

Thiksay Monastery, Ladakh, India.

Part Two: A Deeper Search for Enlightenment

18
FIRST TRIP OUTSIDE MY VILLAGE

I was riding on an overnight bus, and the entire trip would take thirty-two hours. I had wanted to go to Lhasa, but Tashi Lama had only granted me permission to travel north to Gansu province. There are six primary temples for training monks in our line of Buddhism and one of them is in Gansu.

This was my first time on a bus, and I was traveling by myself. I felt out of place. Everyone else on the bus stared at me when I boarded. I was wearing my crimson robes, my head was freshly shaved—and I had on a new pair of black Chinese dress shoes that I had bought at a local market for fifty renminbi, the Chinese currency. I had paid for them with the money Tashi Lama had given to me for the trip. These were the first new shoes I had ever owned. I usually wore hand-me-downs from someone else in my family. For the first ten years of my life, I didn't even have real shoes. My mother would sew together pieces of tough, leatherlike cloth for me to put around my feet to keep them from getting cold or cut up when I ran around the village.

I knew that I was not supposed to be attached to anything in the world, but I loved my new black leather shoes! I couldn't help feeling good in them. Earlier, when I'd seen a small mud puddle that might dirty them, I had stepped to the side. Then, while waiting to board the bus, I had looked down and seen that my shoes were a bit dusty, so I had polished them with the bottom of my robe. I knew that this was wrong. As a monk, I should have felt ashamed of myself for holding something as insignificant as shoes so dear to my heart. However, I had strutted onto the bus, knowing that everyone must be noticing how amazing my new shoes were.

I had just celebrated the Losar New Year festival, which is how we mark our age in Tibet. This festival is like a birthday party for everyone. We do not celebrate individual birthdays, remembering the specific day on which we were born. Instead, we all celebrate our next year of age according to the Losar festival.

For hundreds of years, the Tibetan people have used the New Year festival to calculate their age and to consult with the oracles for the coming years. Every new year, the Nechung Oracle, who is the most senior Oracle and rules together with the Dalai Lama, leads the people in appeasing the water spirits, in order to activate the water elements in our area, and in making smoke offerings to the spiritual world for good fortune.

The bus on which I was riding had two seats on either side of the aisle, four to a row. I walked toward the back of the bus looking for an empty seat. There were several empty window seats toward the front, but with all of them, someone was sitting in the aisle seat next to them. I saw several places toward the back with two empty seats together, so I sat down in an aisle seat and scooted into the spot near the window. I didn't want to miss a moment of what I could see on this journey.

Not long after I sat down, a young lady boarded the bus—and sat in the seat next to me! I pulled my robe toward me so as to not touch her. I was concerned about her sitting beside me, but I didn't want to ask her to leave. She most likely didn't know that it was not possible for me to even touch her. Touching a female could take from me the level of understanding I had achieved.

"Going to Gansu?" she inquired. Her voice was soft and she seemed shy, but that didn't stop her from starting a conversation right away.

"Umm…yes. Gansu. Yes." I had to think about my answer for a moment. It had been more than two years since I had talked to any woman who was not my mother. Tashi Lama forbid us from engaging in conversation with any female. He believed that the smallest interaction with a woman could lead to impure thoughts.

"Do you live there?" she asked, interrupting my thoughts.

"No, but I have been given papers to continue my study," I said as I raised up the papers that had been stamped by Tashi Lama and the local government that allowed me to travel.

"I am going to work at a local nunnery. I have volunteered to work in the sewing room above the restaurant to make special garments."

There were several nunneries close to the male monasteries that operated in this way. Instead of begging for alms every day like the monks did, they made things they could sell to the public.

"Are you a nun?" I asked.

She laughed and leaned forward into her hand to cover her open mouth. "No. I am just a volunteer to help raise money for the nunnery." She sat back up in her seat and regained her composure. "I really admire the dedication of the women who serve there and want to do something to help. I will be married next year and will not have the opportunity to do this again. Who knows? Maybe I will find something during this time to dedicate the rest of my life to. You know," she continued, "I really admire people like you who have dedicated their lives to seeking truth and enlightenment. Like you, I would maybe like to seek truth and be enlightened."

Now I was the one trying not to laugh. A woman finding enlightenment? What a funny thought! Achieving Buddhahood is an extremely rare event. I could hear the words of Tashi Lama echoing in my head: "Women cannot obtain it and can actually create an obstacle for attaining it."

We had been told by monks who had gone out that there were active external forces attempting to change Tibetan Buddhism to allow women to seek enlightenment, but Tibetan beliefs run deep. Genders must be kept separate in their search for enlightenment. Women are considered to be a hellish temptation to the soul and are lower in the cycle of life. They would need to reincarnate at least one more time as a man in order to seek enlightenment.

This had actually been the subject of many passionate lectures in my monastery. Many traveling teachers who visited warned us about this new wave of teaching regarding women being enlightened. I was ready to defend my faith.

The Tibetan system is unapologetically patriarchal, and the idea of equality between the sexes has been incubated in other societies, but not in our culture. Many people mistake Buddhist practices from other parts of China with Tibetan Buddhism. Buddhism in China and other parts of the world is often flavored with values that do not correlate with ours. Enlightenment does not abide by modern rules and is not asexual.

I desperately wanted to share the truth with the young lady sitting beside me. It was clear that she had been misinformed about her place in the world. Buddha himself had been reluctant to expose women to the path to enlightenment because they posed a hindrance to men. I wondered if she knew that he had imposed more rules on them (331 for women compared to 227 rules for men) and made them subordinate to men. I wondered if she knew that Tibetan Buddhist nunneries were not a part of the authority structure for Buddhism.

The Buddha himself said, "Of all the scents that can enslave, none is more lethal than that of a woman. Of all the tastes that can enslave, none is more lethal than that of a woman. Of all the voices that can enslave, none is more lethal than that of a woman. Of all the caresses that can enslave, none is more lethal than that of a woman."

How can you argue with Buddha if you follow him to gain enlightenment? The one who already walked the path can only highlight the path that he took for others to follow. His achievement should be enough to persuade or not persuade.

I wanted to tell her all this, but instead I just sat there. This would be a long ride to Gansu. I didn't want to make enemies before I made any friends. I was not her teacher and she was not seeking my advice. I did not need to persuade her of her errors and she did not need to be persuaded.

These words of Tashi Lama came to me: "Women are the embodiment of samsara." To have argued with this young woman would have been like the endless sequence of *samsara*, the cycle of death and rebirth. Samsara is like a continual wandering in a desert. You never reach your destination. You only walk in circles—over and over again. One can escape this cycle only by achieving enlightenment, or nirvana.

Tashi Lama always said, "Reincarnation is destined for those who do not have enough time in this life to learn their lesson. Reincarnation is for those who are only certain they are right if they can convince others. The path to understanding is lonely, while the path to be right in the eyes of others is circular."

The young woman kept talking, but I was not listening to her. I looked out the window and blocked out her voice. She could not harm what she could not reach, and she could not reach a room guarded by a locked door. As Buddha once said, "Nothing can harm you as much as your own unguarded thoughts."

I always thought that the temptation with women was a sexual one. However, on the bus, I realized that the desire to debate her and educate her was greater than any other desire I had, so I guess the temptation with women had more layers than I realized.

19

BUDDHISM VERSUS ISLAM

Dusk was quickly moving in as our bus roared down Renmin East Road in the sleepy mountain town of Xiahe County in Gansu province. The road grew smaller and smaller as we drove into town—my destination. With small shops on either side, it felt as if the bus was too wide to share the road with any oncoming traffic.

When I climbed off of the bus, stretched my legs, and looked around, I felt that I knew the layout of the town already. It was not really remarkable. The Daxia River was on one side and the mountains with monasteries were on the other. In the middle of the two were the shops and homes of everyone who built their life around the temple.

The streets and shops were full of monks in dark maroon robes and black shoes. Those not wearing robes wore the typical Tibetan jackets lined with warm sheep wool. So, while the faces of those who passed by were not familiar to me, everything else was. The sights, sounds, and smells were all like home. It was as if I knew everything about the town of Xiahe, and it made me wonder if I had been there before.

It was a short walk of about fifteen hundred meters to the Labrang Lamasery temple. The Labrang monastery offered the best chance at accelerating my enlightenment through superior discipleship. This monastery was a treasure house of writings, teachings, paintings, and history preserved through frescoes, tapestries, and architecture. It is one of six of the most important monasteries in Tibetan Buddhism. With its large, blinding white walls, it was easily recognizable as I approached.

"Welcome," said a kind voice from the side of the main stupa. "Are you coming to visit or to join us?"

"Yes, I am here to study," I responded, showing the papers in my hand.

"Oh, we don't need those here," he said. "My name is Melk. Welcome to the Labrang monastery."

Melk looked a little older than I. His face was round and he looked well-fed. He was a little more rotund than the typical monks at my monastery back home.

I looked at the papers in my hand. "I don't need these?" I asked, a bit confused. Tashi Lama had made it very clear to me that I could not study at the Labrang Lamasery without them.

"No. The revelations we teach here are not for sale, nor can they be regulated by a stamp. Those papers are good for the bus ride to Xiahe— nothing more."

I folded the papers and hid them at my side.

Melk squatted down in the typical resting position and motioned for me to join him. "Have you been here before?" he asked me.

"No, I have not. I was sent here by my teacher. He said that I could learn many things here that I would not learn in my own monastery."

"Your teacher is a wise man. There are spirits here that have been leading men down the path of enlightenment for hundreds of years."

"I am excited," I said, pointing out the obvious. "I can't wait to start. I have been dreaming about this place ever since my teacher told me about the history."

"What history have you learned? I am curious."

"Well, I know that it was built by his holiness the Jamyang Shepa, a disciple of the fifth Dalai Lama. It has about ten thousand rooms and three thousand lamas. My teacher told me that this place holds more than sixty thousand sacred sutras."

"Yes, that was mostly correct before the fire in the Great Meeting Hall. What you said is what we share with tourists, but do you know the *real* history of this place?"

I sat silent and waited for him to tell me.

"We are the ancient front line of defense from the Muslim invasion of Tibet. Inside those walls, in a candlelit room, is the two-story-tall golden statue of Tsongkhapa, the founder of our path for all of the Amdo Tibetans. He lights the path that has kept us safe from Islamic invasion in the outer lands for generations." Melk paused for a moment and then continued, "We are at war. The spirits of the gods are active and the demons are prime for an attack."

"War?"

"Yes! War!" he said immediately. "Do not be fooled. The occupation of the Chinese military on Tibetan lands have presented an immediate threat, but the long-term threat is definitely the Muslims."

A strong wind blew against my back, and I shivered.

"Cold?" Melk asked.

I nodded.

"Well, believe it or not, it is warmer out here than inside at the moment. There is no heat. We do not warm up the monastery until November."

It was much colder here in the northern mountains than in my hometown.

"Come," Melk said. "We will get you something much warmer to wear."

As we walked to the monastery, he continued, "While you are here, it is important that you understand that you are not just here as a student. You are a defender. We are the outer walls of the Tibetan people."

"We are?" I asked.

"Mmm," Melk nodded. "There was a time when the Yihewani—also known as the Muslim Brotherhood—launched an attack on our people. Their troops occupied every inch of this monastery. They killed our teachers, destroyed our books, raped our women, and enslaved our children. Jihadi Muslims are the first and only warriors to attempt genocide on our people, but it was our great-grandfathers who eventually repelled their attacks and took back our land from their bloody hands."

Melk was tense. He gritted his teeth as he continued to talk about it. "Did you see them when you arrived?" he asked.

"See who?"

"The Muslims. You will see them everywhere in town. They are outnumbered today, but do not be fooled. They pray to their god several times a day, biding their time. They plot and plan and are waiting for the time to attack again. They long for the days when they ruled over this area and charged all Buddhists that they didn't kill a tax for not converting. Many monks who refused to pay their non-conversion tax were burned to death as a warning to everyone else. Thousands were publicly executed, as commanded by their god in their holy book. The skeletons of our people were scattered far and wide. They were not allowed to be buried. Ten to fifteen skulls were strapped to the horses of common soldiers for decoration and the heads of famous monks hung from the walls of this monastery like a garland of flowers. Today, their merchants will smile to your face to coax you out of your money, but do not think for a moment that they are your friend. They are not. They are your enemy, and you have been sent here to protect your people from them."

I had only just arrived, but I seemed to be learning much. I had never known a Muslim before or even met one, but the province of Gansu was much different from my home province. Melk spent the evening sharing with me that many Hui Chinese people were in Gansu. Hui was a minority group in China that practiced Islam. Another minority group that lived in the surrounding mountains that he particularly stressed were the Dongxiang people. They had their own language and looked completely different from the Chinese or the Tibetans. Most of them could not speak either the Chinese or the Tibetan language and made most of their money in the drug trade. They helped transport drugs from the southern border of China to the western border. They used the funding from the drug trade to support training in their mosques and schools.

The training that they supported made them believe that one day they would once again subjugate the Tibetan people and rule the western highlands of China.

Melk made it a priority to ensure that that day would never come.

20
LULLED TO SLEEP

I lived at the Labrang Lamasery temple in Xiahe County for more than four years, during which time my language facility and knowledge about the scriptures grew by leaps and bounds. However, as I had felt at the monastery in my hometown, I began to feel that I had learned everything there that I could, including from my teacher.

It was true that there were still thousands of texts that I had not seen and there was a constant flow of lamas coming and going. Labrang monastery offered the most complete teaching on Buddhism of any place in China, so my chances of getting a better education or finding a better lama to disciple me were slim. Yet I could not help but feel that there was too much of a focus in Gansu province on liberation from the Chinese occupation. The anti-Islamic fever also flavored much of the teachings. I wondered if our constant resistance against the aggression of the Muslims did not block or at least delay us from obtaining divine understanding.

I thought of Melk, the first monk I had met when I arrived. Even though he had been at the monastery his entire life, I did not think he was any closer to enlightenment than I was. It was quite possible that he wasn't free or enlightened at all, but instead was a slave to his own violent passions against the Muslims.

Melk had a life at the monastery—but maybe not the human life with blood and skin. Instead, maybe he was merely a vessel that gave life to anger. When anger wanted to live, it flowed into his body, and he gave life to the emotion. It lived in him. It flowed through his veins. It occupied his thoughts. It pumped his heart. It was not really the spirit of man that lived in him, but the spirit of anger.

Because of his hatred of Islam, Melk's body was a slave of possession. After several years of knowing him, I did not have the impression that he belonged to himself, but rather to the cause. He was married to the emotion of resisting. The spirit to fight was large and strong and filled his every pore. If he killed it now, it might kill him, because he no longer existed except for the energy of anger that flowed through him.

And I was afraid that I was becoming like Melk.

I didn't mind hating Muslims if hate did not consist of the all-consuming passion that occupied the majority of my thoughts. Unfortunately, it seemed to be the only thing that I could share in common with many of the monks at the monastery. Nothing else seemed to give me passion anymore. All of my interests were dulled and I could not muster the energy to sharpen them.

My weekly debates had become mechanical. I wasn't gaining anything from them and wasn't able to contribute anything through them.

The chanting halls that had excited me when I'd first arrived now did little more than lull me to sleep. Sleep was not what I wanted. Obtaining Buddhahood would require more than just going through the motions. *Buddha* is a title that means "someone who is awake," but living in Labrang no longer made me feel like I was getting any closer to waking up.

From my readings about Buddha, I understood that he never claimed to be a god who could perform miracles. Instead, in the sacred writings that I had read, he spoke of himself as being on a journey of discovery, desiring to know the truth. He constantly spoke of illuminating the path for those who also wished to be awake and understand truth.

Buddha never talked about his family or childhood. He never shared a biography of his life for us to learn more about him personally. His teachings lacked the ramblings of an old man who talks about the "good old days" when he was younger. He was never the focus of his own teachings. Instead, he saw himself as a fellow pilgrim seeking truth.

Buddha's real name, Siddartha, is sometimes translated as "one who obtains his goals" or "one who obtains his desires." His desire was to know the truth. His desire to know the truth called him down various paths in life that required him to leave the comfort of what he knew and to go to places that he did not know. The experiences that led him to his goal were what he shared with his disciples.

Like Buddha, I felt called to leave the comfort of what I knew and go to a place that I did not know. I had come to Labrang monastery to master the ways of Buddha—not to master the ways of protecting myself from Islamic invasion. I did not want to rule over the Muslims and did not want them to rule over me. Ruling over Muslims was elementary compared to ruling over my own soul. If I could learn how to rule my own thoughts, that would truly be a gift from the gods.

Inside, I knew what I had to do. I had to leave the friends I had made in Labrang—some of whom now felt like family—and travel to Lhasa in Southern Tibet. There were a lot of mountains, both physically and metaphorically, between Labrang monastery and Lhasa.

The mountains were high and daunting—beautiful and terrifying at the same time. It was not the mountains that scared me, but the consequences that the mountains could bring about if they were not properly respected and feared. It could even mean death. The mountains themselves did not bring death, but rather the consequences that arose for the one who did not respect the mountains.

However, whatever challenges that might arise from traversing the mountains, staying in Xiahe seemed to be an even greater danger. Obtaining enlightenment at the monastery might very well be impossible because everyone I knew there had not yet obtained it.

How could I keep being discipled by someone who was in their own prison? How could freedom be taught by someone who was not free? How could one teach what one has never known?

I thought about my uncle in Lhasa and what my mother had said about going there. I felt certain it was about time I paid him a visit.

21
LHASA

As I sat on the bus, approaching Lhasa, I was glued to the window. The highway we were traveling was one of the best roads I had ever ridden on.

There seemed to be a light pole every couple of meters. And there were so many cars and people.

Our bus arrived at the Western Station beside the Lhasa River, which ran through the middle of the city. The doors of the bus could not open fast enough for me. I was chomping at the bit. When I stepped down, I took a deep breath and looked around. I had never seen such grandeur and beauty before. There were so many places to go and so many things to see.

To many people, Lhasa might seem like a typical city, with fast food restaurants, massive banks, plush hotels, all-night bars, and office buildings, but to me it was much more than that. It was a holy city that held hidden treasures of history and religion. The gods and goddesses fought with the demons of the underworld and revealed their secrets to men who lived in this city and walked along these alleyways. The voices of past Buddhas whispered across the vortex of time into the ears of millions of seekers, giving riddles of truth and revelation. The map of the city was not just a geographical lexicon of places located in rigid square grids—it was a manual for the ultimate spiritual discovery, where every path leads to a temple or a stone that can give life and understanding.

The name *Lhasa* literally means "land of the gods"—and I had never felt so homesick for a place in my life, even though I had never been there before. I thought that maybe I felt this way because I had been here in another life. Or maybe the spirits that roamed the city streets were ones that I felt at home with. Whatever it was, I was home.

"Momos?" I heard a strange voice call out.

"Yes!" I answered to no one in particular, to which a man yelled back, "Come!"

There was a little stall tucked into the side of a building where Tibetan *momos* were being sold. Its open door was filled with rolling steam. Momos are called the food of the gods. They are exotic steamed dumplings filled with a variety of vegetables, meats, or both. At the counter, they had a wide variety of round- or half-moon-shaped momos to choose from, served piping hot in a Styrofoam container with a side of spicy, tomato-based dipping sauce laced with chutney.

I left the shop with my momos safely secured in both of my hands, and I ate as I strolled. With savory juices flowing over my chin, I tried to take everything in. I was on the "Roof of the World"—where miracles happen. I was not out of place wearing my crimson monk robes. I was surrounded by an entire population of monks who had the ability to separate mind from body and chant the ancient mantras of powerful shamans and mythical oracles.

The further I walked, the thicker the crowds became. I soon found myself wading through throngs of people praying and chanting. They were all facing a variety of altars, which dotted the landscape. I had never seen so many temple-goers in one place before. Years earlier, before I had left home, Tashi Lama had tried to describe this place to me, but everything was grander than he had said.

I continued to stroll along the riverbank on Jinju East Road until I arrived at the location I had waited all of my life to see—the Temple of Mysteries, also known as the Jokhang Temple. Jokhang means "temple of the Lord" and is the resting place of the great statue of Jowo Buddha. The temple is almost a thousand years old and is the center of Lhasa history. It is one of the most important temples in the world for Tibetan Buddhists. For any monk, this temple had to be the first pilgrimage stop in Lhasa. All of the temples are centered on this one location.

As soon as my feet stepped onto the stone of Barkhor Square in front of the temple, I bowed down. Then I stood up again and began walking the *kora* with thousands of other pilgrims. Kora is the meditative ceremony of circling around a holy site in prayer, sometimes performing *gyangchag*—full body prostration—with every step. I could see many pilgrims standing, praying, bowing, then prostrating themselves flat on the ground.

Most major holy sites have koras, and Buddhists can build up holy merit for the afterlife by performing gyangchag as they walk around the koras of the sites. To build up even more merit for the afterlife, they can chant mantras as they prostrate themselves, spin prayer wheels, and count their prayer beads until they reach an auspicious number. Gyangchags are serious business. Some dedicated pilgrims do the full prostration gyangchags from their hometowns—which could be thousands of miles away—all the way to Jokhang Temple.

The prostration starts with your hands folded together in prayer at the *ku*, or the crown of your head, to represent dedication and control of your body. Then, you bring your hands to your *sung*, or mouth, to represent dedication and control of your speech. Next, you bring your hands down to your *thuk*, or heart, to represent dedication and control of your mind. For Tibetans, the heart and mind are one. Then, you bow down to your knees, stretch out your hands in front of your body, and lie down in full prostration. Last, you stand up and start all over again.

Tibetan Buddhists can perform millions of gyangchags over a short period of time in an effort to generate good merit and to pay respect to holy sites—and there were no sites in Tibet more holy than Jokhang Temple. Tibetans believe that Jokhang Temple is one of the twelve holy temples that were needed to subjugate the evil demoness Sinma. The land of Tibet is thought to be formed in the shape of this demoness, who desired to keep Buddhism out of the land so she could run free, terrorizing the people. Four temples were built, called the "Four Horns," as four corners to tie the demoness down at the hips and shoulders. Other temples were built to nail her at the knees and elbows, hands and feet. Jokhang Temple was built to pierce her heart for good measure to ensure her subjugation.

I walked through the crowd of prayer warriors to get to the front entrance of the temple. Some seekers had prepared to pray for so long that they had brought their own mattresses with them. At the entrance, I picked up a container of yak butter to pour into the butter offering lamps. The familiar aroma of these lamps immediately gave me a feeling of spiritual nostalgia.

I tried to squeeze in through the people who were lying prostrate on the floor, blocking the entrance, but it wasn't possible. Nevertheless, the crowd behind me was pushing me forward and I couldn't stop. I tried to place my feet in between people so as not to hurt anyone as I was propelled forward, but a few times, I stepped on people who were praying.

Almost immediately, the environment changed from a spiritual atmosphere to one of mob panic. I was confused and helpless—but also energized. I had never been in such a large crowd before and had never been swept up in so much excitement. I was just a village boy from a rural mountain, but today things were about to change. Now I was in the big capital city of Lhasa—the city of the gods—where dedicated followers from around the world came and formed stampedes to learn from the gods.

Lhasa was even more wonderful than I ever thought it would be. It was scary, exciting, intimidating, and thrilling all at the same time!

22
THE ASSASSINATION

"Why did you come to Lhasa?" my uncle asked. We were walking around Barkhor Square, weaving through people who were praying in front of Jokhang Temple.

I was confused by the question. It seemed very obvious to me—so obvious, in fact, that I didn't even know how to answer him. I had wanted to come because he was my uncle and I was a Buddhist monk. What better place was there for a Buddhist monk to be than Lhasa?

"I want to study the proper form of Buddhadharma," I said. Buddhadharma is the dharma, or teaching, of Buddha and the ultimate way to enlightenment. Dharma is everything. It is the path. It is the truth. It is the essence of everything that a Tibetan Buddhist monk believes.

My uncle looked at me, sighed, and pondered for a moment. "Buddha, Dharma, Sangha," he said in response. "These are the Three Jewels of Buddhism. The Buddha, like you and me, started in the lower realms of hell. He then moved up to the animal realm, the human realm, and the heavenly realm. He was a prince, a family man, a warrior, a beggar, a monk, and finally the Buddha—achieving enlightenment. His path is our refuge, and we must follow his teachings of the dharma.

"We, the community, are the Sangha, and we join together to achieve realization. Our roadblocks are ignorance, anger, attachment, and egotism. Our desire for happiness keeps us from being happy because our desires start with our own ego. Our desire to avoid pain only brings us more pain, because our desires start with our own ego. Do you understand?"

I kind of understood, although not totally. These were all basic concepts of what I had been studying for several years, so I understood what he was saying, but I did not know why he was saying them. I nodded my head up and down to let him know I understood.

"To obtain understanding, you must renounce not only your worldly life, but yourself."

I had already performed the Rite of Chod, so I was familiar with that as well.

"This is the Buddhadharma. You must be in line with the universe, finding your place in the holy order. When the laws of man conflict with the cosmic laws, you must love knowledge more than comfort to follow the cosmic laws."

My uncle looked at me and then glanced over my shoulder—and stopped talking. I turned to see what he was looking at and only saw two men in plain clothes who looked like tourists. He motioned with his head to walk with him to another location, so I followed. As we walked, he continued in a hushed voice, "Listen very carefully to me, because I do not know how long I have to share with you."

"What? Why?" I asked.

"Shhh...listen carefully. There are Three Principal Aspects of the Path. The Three Principal Aspects are renunciation, bodhicitta, and emptiness. Bodhicitta is the enlightened mind, but not just any enlightened mind. It is the mind that is enlightened for the good of others and desires to enlighten others."

I was still confused. What my uncle was telling me was not a big secret. This was basic Buddhism 101.

"Bodhicittas do not just seek truth. They are shepherds who give their life to ensure that the sheep arrive at their destination safely. But sometimes the shepherds are attacked by wolves that desire the meat of the sheep." He turned and looked at me sternly. "Are you ready to be a shepherd?"

Again, the two men in common clothes approached us. My uncle put his head down and walked briskly in a different direction. I tried to follow closely behind him to continue our conversation, but his pace was so fast that I almost felt like I would have to break into a slow jog. Then my uncle leaned toward me and said, "PSB," referring to the men who seemed to be following us. PSB means Public Security Bureau. It is China's version of the CIA in America or the KGB in Russia.

We had turned the corner in an alley and taken a couple of steps when my uncle pulled me into a small restaurant stall. We walked through the eating area and into the kitchen, and then exited through the back door. I found myself walking down another street with my uncle, away from the men from the PSB.

"I do not know how much longer we will know peace in Lhasa," my uncle said. "The wolves are coming for the sheep, and the shepherds will need to sacrifice to protect the sheep." Then he stopped, looked at me, looked down at the ground, and then looked back up at me before saying, "I believe that the Panchen Lama has just been assassinated—killed by the government."

For my tribe, the Panchen Lama was the holiest person in the world and second in power only to the Dalai Lama. In fact, the Panchen Lama chooses the Dalai Lama when he reincarnates and the Dalai Lama chooses the Panchen Lama when he reincarnates.

"Why would they kill him?" I asked. The Panchen Lama had shared power with the Dalai Lama in Tibet during the Cultural Revolution in China when Mao Zedong came to power. But when the Dalai Lama escaped to India and protested the Chinese occupation of Tibet, the Panchen Lama supported the rise of the Communist Party and their occupation under the guise of liberation. He was made chairman of the Party for the Autonomous Region of Tibet—which was the highest position of power.

"Because they cannot allow him to live," my uncle responded. "Ever since he publicly denounced the Party's treatment of Tibetans, they have punished him and tried to get him to take back his words. They labeled him an "enemy of the state" and sent him to prison. When he got out of prison, he left the monastery. The government arranged for him to marry the daughter of a Chinese Army general, and they had a daughter together."

Arranged marriages were common in Communist China. It was how Mao Zedong attempted to secure his power in minority areas. The daughter of the Panchen Lama was very special to Tibetans, affectionately known as the "Princess of Tibet." She is the only known child of any Panchen Lama in over six hundred years, and for that reason she is also sometimes called "The Buddha's Daughter."

"The Buddha's Daughter was sent out of the country to live with a famous American actor named Steven Seagal, so her safety is secure, but his own life has been in danger."

"They killed him?"

"Yes. He was assassinated. The government hit men made it look like a heart attack."

I stopped. This was shocking news for me as a Tibetan monk. The most important religious leader in Tibet had just been killed by the Chinese government.

"The Chinese government now considers it to be within their power to select the new Panchen Lama."

"What!" I yelled.

"Shhhhh…you mustn't draw attention to yourself."

"The Chinese government is atheist! How can atheists possibly know how to choose a living Buddha?" I asked.

"Now is not the time to lose your head. Now is the time to decide—will you be a shepherd or a sheep? Things are not going to get easier after today. Are you ready to be a real Bodhicitta?"

23
JOINING THE RESISTANCE

Early in the morning, I left the monastery where I was staying in Lhasa and headed out to pray along the kora around Jokhang Temple, but it was a difficult process. There were blocks and checkpoints on the way there and even around the kora.

Since the assassination of Panchen Lama, there had been an uneasiness in the air. Protests, both big and small, were taking place almost daily. Marshall law had been declared in the city of Lhasa, and I felt like I was living in a military compound. I started to notice an increase of security everywhere. Convoys of military trucks flooded the city. There were more and more of them every day. Men dressed in olive green military uniforms mixed with monks in maroon robes in Barkhor Square. Military units set up checkpoints on all the main roads to look for weapons. Snipers took up positions on rooftops around the city. I couldn't go anywhere without being watched or frisked. The airport was shut down and foreigners were not allowed to visit. It was against the law for any monk to be caught talking to the foreign press. Newspapers and TV newscasts didn't report on the unrest in Tibet at all.

Lhasa was not the only place experiencing problems with protests. Rumors were rapidly spreading that a Chinese military commander who had recommended that the Chinese should allow Tibet to be free had just died in the same suspicious way that Panchen Lama had. A hundred thousand people had showed up at his funeral and led a protest at Tiananmen Square for democracy.

The police brutality that I witnessed in Lhasa surprised me at first. Eventually, my surprise turned to fear, but now that fear was turning into hatred. I could feel it bubbling up inside of me. My anger increased every time I was stopped and frisked. The Chinese soldiers, many of whom were only teenagers, delighted in pushing me around and pulling on my robes as they checked me.

"Here, take this," one of the shop owners in the market said as I stepped away from the guard post. She secretly slipped me a leaflet. Such leaflets were protests of the Chinese occupation in Tibet and were written in English and Tibetan. They were most likely printed in India or Nepal because the quality was much better than anything one could buy in Tibet or China. However, the leaflets were not informative—they just repeated slogans.

Resistance was quickly becoming the new mantra. Even in the monasteries, we were hearing teachings and sermons about active resistance against the Chinese government. The government believed that the top percent of privileged people held power and implemented religion and culture in order to exploit the lower classes of people and minorities. It was clear that they saw us monks as a part of the power structure at the top. They believed that the minds of the people had been poisoned over the course of thousands of years. To be "liberated," they needed to be cleansed of what were called the Four Olds: Old Customs, Old Culture, Old Habits, and Old Ideas.

We were the enemy.

Chinese government officials are not elected. They are communists and answer to the party, not the people. The government officials who were at the top of the chain of command in Lhasa had been sent by Beijing. They were not even from Tibet. They did not speak the language or understand the culture. The Communist Party of China strongly adheres to the basic teachings of Karl Marx, who said that "religion is the sigh of the oppressed creature, the heart of a heartless world, and the soul of soulless conditions. It is the opium of the people." These words had been emphasized by Mao Zedong and made it impossible for the government officials to understand or respect our religious practices.

The Chinese government started the process of trying to remove everything that made Tibetans unique. Communists do not like unique. Their ideal society is one that makes everyone the same. They want everyone to think the same and live the same. They want men and women to dress the same. They wanted Tibetans to abandon their heritage and laws and to adopt the modern society of new China. They wanted us monks to trade in our monastic robes for Mao suits.

The Tibetan people were losing control of their lives, and they felt helpless. They thought their culture and religion were being ripped from them—and they were not wrong. They turned to the monks for help. The Drepung Monastery was the most active in the protests. Drepung, just on the outskirts of Lhasa, is the largest Tibetan Buddhist monastery in the world, with as many as ten thousand monks at any given time.

Barkhor Square quickly became ground zero for resistance against the Communist regime. The symbolism of Barkhor Square and Jokhang Temple was not obvious to the Chinese military commanders. Jokhang Temple had been built to subdue the evil demoness by the Fifth Dalai Lama, who had brought peace, but now that peace was being threatened. The Chinese soldiers unwittingly walked counterclockwise, against the crowds praying around the kora. When a Buddhist prays around the kora, they should be in a state of extreme peace and submission, but the soldiers carried guns. Even the most compliant Tibetans were being pushed to their limits by the offenses brought on by the Chinese military and the open disrespect for the most holy sites.

The monks from Drepung Temple used the kora around Jokhang Temple for the central planning of their protests because it was a place where most Tibetans came every day. The kora, meant for praying and building up points for the afterlife, was the most effective way to reach the most people with illegal messages. The dissident community that protested against the occupation of China touched every stratum of Tibetan society, from students to merchants, from farmers to clerks, and from monks to drunks.

The government had wanted to reform Tibet in an attempt to create a more perfect Communist state. They were certain that they knew better than we did and could do what was best if they could only control everything about our lives. However, in the end, it conceived the birth of a Buddhist revival that gave Tibetans a cause and a national identity.

Protests were breaking out on a weekly basis. Monks were being shot by the police. Those who were not shot were put on public trial at the sports stadium in Lhasa. For dramatic effect, executions were announced as the accused were led out of the stadium. It was a shot across the bow of the Tibetan agitators.

Attendance at the public trials at the stadium was required for government workers and schoolchildren. Government officials lectured the crowds on the need for stability and mindfulness, and of the benefits of communism for the poor.

Earlier, there had been protests at a police station where several monks had been taken after being arrested. The protestors marched in front of the police station and started to wave makeshift Tibetan flags. The protests turned violent and eventually the jail was set on fire. A Tibetan monk named Champa Tenzin ran into the burning police station and unlocked the jail cells to release the imprisoned monks. Some of the monks were shot and killed as they ran out, but Champa Tenzin became an instant hero. He was hoisted on the shoulders of the protesters and praised for his bravery before he fled Tibet.

The Chinese were so angry after this incident that they banned the Tibetan New Year celebration—the largest holiday of the year. Things got so bad that China's President Jiang Zemin made a special trip to Lhasa and personally tried to calm the situation. He promised more free subsidies for the people of Tibet. What he failed to realize is that we did not want free subsidies. We wanted freedom.

We did not want his promise of greater economic prosperity where government-owned enterprises came with bulldozers and dynamite to destroy the traditions of shepherding, farming grasslands, and traditional horseback riding.

We did not want our mountains raped of copper, silver, and oil.

We did not want to be monitored all the time by the government. We wanted to be left alone.

If the Chinese people wanted to be Red Communists, then they were free to make that decision, but we had different ideas. We wanted China to keep out of the religious affairs of the Tibetan people. We wanted the freedom to teach our children in school in their own native tongue. We wanted the freedom to travel and learn at other monasteries without written permission by the government. And we didn't want to be forced to openly denounce our most important religious leader, the Dalai Lama.

In short, we chose a theocracy, not communism. Our leader was the Dalai Lama, not Jiang Zemin. In our eyes, Communist China was the very thing that they claimed to resist: it was a colonizer.

Although I never took any action other than being in the crowds of protestors, that was enough for the government to consider me a part of the resistance. Moreover, as a monk, I was automatically linked to the opposition against Chinese occupation.

24
FEEDING YOURSELF TO THE TIGRESS

The protests continued, and every week seemed to be a repeat of the last. The resistance against the Chinese government had a flavor similar to what I had experienced in the Muslim areas of Gansu province. Different enemy, same spirit of resistance.

Every protest in Lhasa started and ended the same way. First, on the night prior to a protest, several monks would secretly meet together and pray to the protector goddess Palden Lhamo, the patron deity of Tibet and the Dalai Lama. The monks would make a vow never to betray each other if caught. If necessary, they would sacrifice their own lives before giving up information about the others. For a monk, such an oath before the gods was stronger than any written contract.

Next, they would walk to the Nechung Monastery and make a burnt offering of juniper leaves, a ritual to pacify the gods and earn their favor for the conflict to come. The following day, they would arrive at Jokhang Temple and walk the kora, sharing their plans with others. As soon as the crowds were big enough, they would unfurl large, handmade, cotton flags representing Tibet and start shouting slogans about Tibetan independence. After some time, nuns would join in the chanting.

Before long, the military units would arrive in riot gear. They would run into the crowds with gas masks and start clubbing, kicking, and striking every monk they could find. In Africa, when lions chase bovine, they create a stampede, and then the stragglers are separated from the herd and feasted on by the swarming pride. The police used a similar method. They would start arresting individual monks and sending them to large vehicles able to hold dozens of prisoners at a time. Some arrests did not involve handcuffs but instead metal cords that were wrapped around the neck of the monk by the arresting officer, putting them in a choke hold.

Then they would link the neck cord to the monk's hands behind his back. The police attacks and brutal arrests would provoke the crowds who were merely observing. Large, unruly crowds of Tibetans would then join in the protests and clash with the police.[5]

Following this, the police, with only a few protestors in cuffs—usually monks—would retreat to the local jail. Finally, the demonstrators would follow the police down Renmin Lu (The People's Road) and protest in front of the police station until the mob grew tired and retired for the evening.

It was the same story every single time. There was an undeniable rhythm to it that was shamefully predictable. For the most part, the riots were not really effective. They were not deterring the Chinese government in the least from doing what they wanted to do and when they wanted to do it.

On March 28, 1959, China had officially declared the Tibetan government illegal. According to the Chinese government, that is the day they emancipated the Tibetans from the controls of religion and serfdom (and into the controls of the communist government).[6] Thirty years later, in 1989, Tibetans were still rejecting their "emancipation," but their choices were very limited. They did not have the ability to vote the communists out of power because China was not a democratic nation. They did not have the weapons or the power to repel the Chinese military police because personal weapons had been banned in Tibet. They did not have a voice in the media because journalists had been banned from Lhasa.

Some Tibetans grew so tired of the violence and fighting that they began to give in and submit to the virtual slavery of the Chinese government. A number of monks were sent to reeducation camps where they were beaten and tortured and brainwashed to think like a communist. Most of them died in the reeducation camps, and those who did not physically die left the camps as only a shell of a human being. Their body was present, but their spirit was gone.

---

5. Raw video of the 1989 Tibetan clashes can be seen at https://www.youtube.com/watch?v=jBxvhrWy0FI.

6. In 2009, the Tibetan legislature declared March 28 to be an annual holiday called "Tibetan Emancipation of Serfs Day."

Worst of all, the children of Tibet suffered. They did not really have a chance to learn the language, culture, and heritage of the Tibetan people. There was a general fear that the next generation of children would be controlled by the government and would no longer know their rich heritage.

In order to achieve some kind of normalcy in their lives, the majority of Tibetan parents in Lhasa would send their children to Chinese schools. Although the parents would protest during the day, at the same time, their children would be in classrooms run by Han Chinese, being taught that Communist China had brought liberation to Tibet. It was like we were sacrificing our own children.

There was an overwhelming feeling of helplessness. We had no voice or power to change anything.

Tibetan families were suffering, and it was clear that protests were not getting us anywhere. A different approach to protesting was needed if we wanted to gain the attention of the rest of the world, so a few of the monks started to take more drastic measures, measures that were more controversial. they began to share about self-immolation—the act of publicly killing oneself as a sacrifice.

I heard about a story from the ancient writings of the Jatakas. The Jatakas are holy literature in Buddhism detailing the previous lives of the Buddha in both animal and human form. In one of the stories, he gave his life to benefit the lives of animals. In that incarnation, Buddha was a (different) prince who came across a starving tigress and her cubs. The tigress was so hungry that she was ready to eat her own offspring. In order to save the dignity and purity of the mother tiger, the prince threw himself off of a cliff and killed himself so that the tigress and her cubs could have something to eat. In doing so, he did not die but rather came closer to perfection. His disciples rejoiced because, through a compassionate sacrifice, he found a new truth in greater morality. This event is often depicted in paintings showing a tigress eating the Buddha.

Tibetan lamas began to use this story in their teachings as an illustration of the ultimate gift of compassion for those who lived under the tyranny of Chinese occupation. Monks began to discuss the act of burning themselves in a show of resistance. Plans were laid for monks to publicly swallow fragrant wood chips and wrap their body in ceremonial cloth that had been doused in flammable oil. They could then march to the central square in Lhasa and set themselves on fire. The fire would burn the oil on their robes, and the wood chips would give a scent of sacrifice that would be pleasing to the gods. In this way, the tigress, hungry for freedom, would not have to eat her own cubs.

The message of the lamas was crystal clear: if we did not want the Tibetan people to eat their own cubs, we would have to offer ourselves as a sacrifice.

25
ABHIDHARMA: THE HIGHEST DHARMA

With my right hand of enlightenment, I smacked down hard against my left hand of doctrine in front of the defender Dawa, one of the fellow monks at the monastery, and waited for his response.

"I accept," he said with a smile.

I think he was smiling because it was not easy to even hear what I was saying. There were so many monks standing all around us, debating with one another, practicing defending their theories, and no doubt making up new ones of their own.

Every week, you could be sure to see all of the monks from our monastery out debating with one another. The sound from our courtyard was a loud cacophony of lecturing, yelling, and clapping. We debated with each other as if we were debating in the great Samye Debate, also known in Tibetan Buddhism as the Council of Lhasa, where two Buddhist monks spent two years debating one another in front of a Tibetan king in the eighth century.

"Concentrate," said my uncle from the background. He was somehow able to hear through the noise and distractions of the other people debating and zero in on exactly what we were saying. It was almost as if no one else in the world existed except for the two of us and that we were performing only for him.

"You are the embodiment of Manjusri! Manjusri is the embodiment of wisdom, and his right hand has a flaming sword, cutting down ignorance and duality. So, when you bring down your right hand, strike your left hand so hard that the world quakes with the destruction of ignorance."

The words of my uncle sank in. I turned my body away from Dawa and then back to him, again clapping my hands as hard as I could while bringing down my foot in a stomp that shocked the bones in my heel.

"And it was then that the colors that came out of his body were blue, yellow, red, white, orange, and a mixture of these five," I said. "The mixture of the five colors represented the most noble qualities of enlightenment. The colors that shined did not shine before Buddha was enlightened. The colors came out of his body only after his enlightenment." I ended my phrase by striking my hands together and stomping my right foot at the same time.

"I accept," Dawa said. Again, I was not certain if he could even hear everything that I said because of the surrounding noise, but it would have been easy for him to follow since I was quoting the events of the Abhidharma. The Abhidharma is a collection of the highest and purest teachings of Buddhism.

"The six colors reflected the wisdom, the highest wisdom, of the highest Dharma, which he gained from visiting the second realm of heaven— the last level that connects the heavenly realm with the earthly realm."

With that phrase, I stopped. For the first time, instead of just remembering the Abhidharma, I began to really digest what it meant.

"So must we visit the second heavenly realm and climb to the Peak of Sumeru to obtain enlightenment?" I posed the question, but I did not gesture for Dawa to confirm. I was actually asking the question of myself. "Is Abhidharma all around me, or must I seek it only in the heavens? If it is simply all around, then why didn't Buddha merely teach us to take it from the air that we breathe? And if Abhidharma is found only in the heavens, then what keeps me bound to the earth?"

Both Dawa and my uncle looked at me like puzzled kittens.

"What are we searching for? Are we searching for Abhidharma or the effects of Abhidharma? Do we simply wish for the colors of Abhidharma on earth to show to men or do we strive for the knowledge of Abhidharma that apparently comes only from heaven? Am I spending my entire life searching the world for the supreme wisdom that cannot be found on earth?"

I didn't clap. I didn't spin. I didn't stomp my foot. I was dumbfounded by the sudden uselessness of it all. If heaven was the source of Abhidharma, then what did I ever hope to accomplish with a debate on earth? "Do we seek Abhidharma or do we imitate the act of seeking?"

"Finished," yelled my uncle, prematurely stopping the debate. "That is enough for today."

"No. Not yet."

Dawa looked up at me in a state of shock. My uncle was breaking protocol by not allowing me to finish the debate. The debate was not considered to be finished until I shouted, "Finished!" three times and clapped my hands together as hard as I could. Yet a disciple never questions his teacher, even if the teacher is breaking the rules of a debate.

"My goal is not to win a debate with you, Dawa. It never was." The words were being formulated in my mouth as fast as they were taking shape in my mind. There was no filter. "This debate is supposed to destroy the false design of reality that keeps us from obtaining truth. Truth is a treasure and we are the explorers. Our aim is to find it. If we do not find it, we can always debate what we did find, but we should never feel free to create that which we did not find. We are painters painting only what we see, not painting what we do not see."

I thought about that analogy for a moment and expanded on it just a bit. "If I were a painter and wanted to paint a different scenery, would it make sense to paint it only from someone else's experience? Wouldn't that be inferior to painting it from the inspiration of my own experience? How can I debate Abhidharma, revealed to Buddha from heaven, if I have never been to heaven? Will the five colors of wisdom emanate from me if I experience heaven only through someone else?"

I felt like I was knocking on the door of intellectual liberation—but only for a moment. My uncle was losing patience with me. I had made him lose face in front of Dawa, and I knew that this would not easily be forgotten.

But everything in my life sat in front of me in that suspended moment. I had already spent several years in the monastery studying the dharma of Buddha and being taught the ultimate components of existence. I had read, chanted, prayed, prostrated, meditated, and fasted from food and water for countless days with the fleeting hope that I could catch a glimpse of understanding. "If heaven is where we will find the supreme dharma, then why do we always seem so far away?" I asked.

"We are finished for today," my uncle said again, this time more sternly. His authority was not to be tested.

Dawa put his head down and stared at the ground. I think he felt ashamed for my sake.

Even though I felt the fear of what might happen with my uncle, I walked away knowing that something was shaking inside of me that would contribute to a breakthrough.

26
THE SEARCH FOR ABHIDHARMA

Enlightenment is power—but I felt powerless. The more I learned, the more ignorant I felt. Tibetan Buddhism has so many writings, so many gurus, and such a long history. Not only were there a plethora of things to learn from our written canons, but there were also secret dharmas that could only be found through continual revelation.

I prayed for the power of Buddha to help me obtain enlightenment. I yearned for the awakening of my true nature, which could understand all knowledge, both past and future.

According to Tibetan Buddhist belief, there are ten powers, so I silently prayed for all ten. "I pray for the power over life. I pray for the power over my mind. I pray for the power over material things. I pray for the power over my actions. I pray for the power over birth. I pray for the power over desire. I pray for the power over prayer. I pray for the power over miracles. I pray for the power over wisdom. I pray for the power over dharma."

On the advice of my uncle, I had left the monastery and begun a pilgrimage all around Tibet. I traveled day and night, going from one village to the next and staying in various monasteries. I lived at the Sera Temple and watched the great debates where some of the most famous Tibetan monks come out every day to challenge one another with their knowledge of scriptures.

I traveled to each of the main monasteries in Lhasa. I made my way to the Potala Palace, one of the most beautiful places I have ever been to in my life, and I walked around with several other monks and prayed. On the day I was there, the ashes of the former Dalai Lamas were on display. The other monks whom I was with said that they could feel closer to enlightenment by being closer to the ashes of the Dalai Lamas, but I didn't feel any significant difference.

Behind the Potala Palace is a small temple known as the Secret Temple, where the Dalai Lama would meditate. It is full of murals showing details of long-forgotten practices. It is the place that commemorates the submission of Naga, the King Snake, to the great Guru Rinpoche, who helped build the first Buddhist monastery in Tibet.

I trekked to Yerpa Temple and joined my fellow monks in a few days of meditation in the ancient caves just outside of Lhasa.

I made my way to Tradruk Monastery in Yarlung Valley, which was founded by the great king Songsten Gampo, who founded Tibet and the Tibetan written language, and who brought Buddhism to our people.

I traveled to each of the other temples that had been built to hold down the evil demoness Sinma. I went to Tashi Lhunpo Temple in Shigatse, which was founded by the very first Dalai Lama. I continued along the Southern Friendship Highway to the Drongtse Monastery, which had mostly been destroyed by the Chinese, but still had several monks there teaching, praying, and meditating.

I made my way to the sacred Lotus Chrystal Cave, not far from the Dzongsar Monastery, a place that had been visited by the Guru Rinpoche.

I stayed at each monastery for only a few days and then moved on. Each temple that I visited was fascinating and full of its own gods, goddesses, teachings, and relics. A few temples were in places in which I could see myself staying for several years, but I had an internal tug that kept pulling me onward. I had to keep trekking and searching.

I didn't know exactly what I was searching for other than total enlightenment of the Abhidharma. I thought that I might know it when I saw it. I found all of the sacred places that I was visiting spiritually titillating, but I lacked satiation. I was hungry for more than what I was finding.

The biggest challenge that I found in most monasteries is that they lacked peace. They were all fighting something. They were fighting either the oppressive Communist Party or the ghosts of the past. The temple in Gansu where I had served was opposed to the Muslims. The temple in Lhasa was fighting against the Chinese occupation. This lack of peace caused stress, and I could sense it at each of the temples I visited. Meditations and prayers were interrupted by local opposition by the Chinese authorities. I saw that each temple in Tibet was unified in turmoil.

As I toured the monasteries in Tibet, I was also learning that the Tibetan Buddhist experience was a bloody one. This was not just in relation to their resistance against invading forces, but there was an extremely violent history of fighting between Buddhists in Tibet that went back over a thousand years. The violence was not just in our everyday lives, but it was in our history. And it was not just in our history, but it was in our religion. I began to think that perhaps violence was in our blood, because it seemed to follow us everywhere. Even though I had been taught to seek peace and tranquility, everything seemed full of trials and hardships.

One of the most holy sites in Tibet is a small body of water in the mountains known as Lhamo Latso Lake. It is an extremely sacred lake for my people where the oracles come to seek visions that can point them to the reincarnation of the Dalai Lama. The lake is named after a spiritual goddess, Palden Lhama. Palden Lhamo is the principal protector of the Tibetan people and of our lamas, like the Dalai Lamas and Panchen Lamas.

Even though the Tibetan people pray to Palden Lhamo as a protector, she is actually extremely wrathful. Her image is always angry and her fury is represented by an all-consuming fire that continually surrounds her. Her story is one of vile rampage and bloodshed. Palden Lhamo was married to the king of Lanka, who would not accept the Buddhist religion. The goddess tried many times to convert him, but he would not accept. In her anger at her failed attempts to convert the king, she killed her own son while her husband was out hunting. Then she ate her son's flesh, drank his blood from his skull, and flayed his skin to make a saddle for her horse before fleeing from her kingdom and heading north toward Tibet.

Palden Lhamo eventually died and went to hell, but in her anger, she fought her way out of hell carrying a bag of diseases and a sword. She swore to use her diseases and sword to fight against the enemies of the reincarnation of the Dalai Lamas.

She also appeared to King Gampo, the founder of Tibet, and promised him that if he would erect an image of her to be worshipped, she would protect his royal shrine from future damage by man.

I thought of her image, the one that we prayed to. It was not an image that invoked peace or kindness. It was one that conjured up images of hate, anger, and wrath. Palden Lhamo is often depicted in temples in the following ways: with fiery red hair, to symbolize her vengeful nature; crossing a sea of blood; or riding sidesaddle on her mule. She is using the skin of her dead son as a saddle blanket and is often shown drinking his blood from his skull.

"Our people look to her for protection?" I asked myself. "She is celebrated for slaughtering her own son and drinking his blood."

The goddess Palden Lhamo was not alone in her violent nature. Almost all of the gods and goddesses that we prayed to and sought guidance from had extremely violent stories to tell. I thought back to the images from my early childhood of the angry, man-sized monkey with the evil red face, holding a sword, which our family had on the entrance to our home. I remembered how the sword of the monkey god was covered with the blood pouring down from the neck of the woman whom he had killed. That murderous monkey was honored as the ancestor of our people.

Could it be that our present violence was linked to our gods and goddesses in Tibet? It was confusing to me. How could I expect to find Abhidharma in the midst of such turmoil and brutality?

I decided that Tibet might not be the best place for me to find the highest form of enlightenment. It was time for me to travel to the place of Buddhism's earliest history.

27
LEAVING TIBET

The night wind sweeping down from the mountains felt so crisp and clean in my lungs when I inhaled. I wanted to take in this moment because it was a moment like no other—I was leaving Tibet to go on a trip in hopes of studying under *the Dalai Lama*. The trip would have to be taken in secret in order to avoid detection by the Chinese officials. We would hike during the night and sleep during the day so we could keep undercover.

"Circle around me," Joha said. Joha was the guide who would help us navigate through the mountains between China and India. He had made the trip many times and knew the back trails. My uncle had introduced me to Joha after it was decided that I should travel to India to continue my studies.

"As we travel, it is important that everyone stays together. If anyone falls away from the group, they might get lost and die, so you must stay close to me. The journey will be about a month long and will not be easy for any of us. If you are having second thoughts, now is the time to opt out. You will not be able to come back after we start."

We all looked around at each other and remained silent for a few moments to see if there was anyone who did not want to go. No one seemed to want to stay. Besides, we had all paid our fee of more than one thousand Chinese yuan per person. That was a lot of money for us. It was more than some of the people in the group could make in a year.

"OK," Joha said as he reached back, picked up his backpack, and slung it over his shoulders. "Here we go. Follow me." There was a quiet shuffle as we slowly peeled off from our huddle to follow him. There were twenty-one of us altogether—including a mother carrying her baby—and we made a long line into the night.

Joha was easy to follow, even through the darkness of the night, because he was dressed in bright, shiny colors. He had all of the latest hiking clothing. His clothing looked like it would repel water and hold in heat. Definitely not from Tibet. Tibetan handmade clothing was thick and bulky with dull, neutral colors that blended in well with the surroundings. In addition, Joha's nylon backpack was noticeably lighter than ours and had most likely come from America or a European country. It looked expensive.

All I had to keep me warm was my robes. I was not even wearing shoes. I'd had to leave my shoes in the monastery so as not to alert anyone of my absence too early. Only my uncle knew that I was going. However, I was not worried about my lack of shoes because my feet had had years of toughening. I'd spent my entire childhood hiking around the mountainside without shoes. The mountains were my home, and I didn't need anything more than what I had on my back.

All of us started out with full bellies and lots of excitement. The first night of hiking, the group just bounced along. Once we got far enough away from Lhasa, we began to sing famous Buddhist scriptures. My heart leapt with adventure—and I sang the loudest. We did not have a care in the world. Joha had planned stops along the way where we could get resupplied with food and water. He had been on the trail many times and knew exactly how far we needed to hike every evening.

When we would get close to a village, Joha would stop along a mountain ridge and shout out a hooting sound of greeting that would bounce off of the sides of the rocky cliffs. After shouting, he would pause for a moment and shout again, waiting for a response from a caller from the village.

I felt that our voices carried further during the evening, so at one point, I walked up to Joha and squatted down beside him. I could barely make out his image in the night, but his colorful clothing reflected what little moonlight there was. "Aren't you concerned about government officials finding out that we are here?" I asked curiously.

Joha laughed. "Government officials out here?" He laughed again. Even in the dimness, I could see him shaking his head. "Trust me. The officials that the government has assigned over this region have never been out here. There is no worry about that."

Joha was able to shout to certain villages along the way because he was acquainted with and trusted the particular callers who would be answering. We heard a loud hooting call like that of an owl being returned from the village below. After Joha heard the call, we continued along the ridge line.

"Are we not going down to the village?" I asked.

"No, it is too risky," Joha replied.

"What do you mean? I thought that the government officials did not come to the villages out here. What is the risk?"

"The villagers cannot know who we are. It will take us almost another month to cross the border into Nepal. There might not be any officials here, but villagers are loudmouths. They talk about everything when they start drinking their rice wine. If the villagers travel into town and talk about our smuggling trail, then the police might be able to intercept us at the border or prohibit us from returning in the future. The fewer people who know about what we are doing, the better." With that, Joha kept walking.

After that evening, our energy levels decreased little by little. Although we had dried barley noodles to snack on from time to time, we didn't have much more than raw barley to chew on to sustain us in our journey.

Joha had reserves of turnips and potatoes that he carried with him, but he rationed them out so that the supply would last for the entire journey. Every two days, he would give us dried pork, which was kept in pig intestines, so that we could have a bit of protein in our diet.

Dried meat is common in the Chinese diet, but not as common for a Tibetan monk to eat. The Chinese do not ever eat anything raw. They like to cook, fry, or cure their meats, whereas we like to have meat with the blood still in it. Eating dried pork for several weeks was not going to be an easy task for me.

The songs that we sang for the first few nights were slowly replaced with silence. We did not have much more to sing about. Our feet were sore, our legs and backs were tired, and our stomachs felt empty.

Because I was a monk, I was more used to being hungry for long periods of time than many of the other people in the group. Every month, the monks would spend time fasting—we would fast on the eighth, tenth, fifteenth, twenty-first, and thirtieth. During that time, I would meditate and pray. I would also meditate, fast, and pray for long periods during special holidays and meditations.

Nyungne fasting is the Tibetan ritual of fasting for several days. For me, Nyungne fasting was an act of cleansing. Nyungne is not just about denying food to the body. It is a ceremony of strict vows that involves long periods of silence and meditation, in addition to going without food. Tibetan Buddhists believe that Nyungne fasting purifies the soul and brings healing to the body. Thus, even though I was hungry and often tired and miserable during the hike, I believed that the forced fasting was good for my soul.

Over the next several nights, as we hiked in silence, I tried to think about anything that did not involve my desire to eat. I stopped concentrating on the lack of food and repeated to myself the Eight Precepts, which are the vows that every Tibetan monk makes in order to help them obtain Abhidharma:

I make a solemn vow against killing.

I make a solemn vow against stealing.

I make a solemn vow against sexual impurity.

I make a solemn vow not to lie.

I make a solemn vow to abstain from drugs.

I make a solemn vow to maintain fasting.

I make a solemn vow to rid myself of personal indulgences.

I make a solemn vow to stay clear of placing myself in prideful positions.

I used the prayer beads in my hand to help me keep track of the number of times I made the prayer, and for a number of nights, reciting the Eight Precepts to myself helped take my mind off of the pain. However, after a week without real food, I was losing my willpower to keep going.

28
"I CAN'T GO ON ANY LONGER"

We were all suffering and did not want to continue, but Joha kept pushing us to keep moving. After a couple of weeks of traversing through the unforgiving mountains, the border of Nepal and Tibet didn't seem any closer than it had when we left from Lhasa. We had been walking like zombies through the night, and we did not appear to be making any progress. We no longer had much energy to walk because none of us were really getting any sleep during the day.

The lack of oxygen in the mountains was also taking its toll. Due to the high altitude, I was feeling sensations in my body that I had never felt before. There was tingling in my fingertips and lips. My mouth felt like it was full of cotton. My head pounded with an aching pain that synchronized with my own heartbeat. Every step that I took used as much energy as if I were running at a lower altitude.

Joha announced that we would not be getting oxygen pillows on this trip. In past trips, he had arranged stops along the route that allowed everyone to sleep with these pillows during the day. Oxygen pillows are bags filled with oxygen that are fitted with a tube that you can suck on to take in extra air. Oxygen pillows are essential as one's body acclimates to a higher altitude. Unfortunately, because of security problems, Joha had to cancel visiting the Tibetan villages that provided pilgrims with oxygen pillows.

We had also run lower on food than we expected. Thus, everyone, down to the last person, was immersed in a smog of dizzying exhaustion.

A dense blanket of a fear of death was beginning to loom over us, and I could not chase it away. I became convinced that none of us would make it out alive.

At one point, we had to walk half a week through desert regions with very little water, and at another point, we had to walk another half a week through damp, swampy regions where nothing ever stayed dry.

Along the trail, there were areas where we could barely walk because the path was so narrow and hard to see at night. Once, I lost my footing and fell several feet down a cliff, almost plunging to my death, but I was able to catch a branch and pull myself up.

Wild, nocturnal animals always surrounded us, waiting for us to lose our way and become separated from the group. Whenever we stopped, we could hear the wolves howling close by.

I stopped praying and chanting. It was not doing any good. The fog of fear was so tangibly thick that my mind was no longer able to pierce it with meditation alone. The mountains of Tibet, which had once been my place of refuge and placidity, were now my nemeses.

Two nights earlier, the mother who was carrying her baby was not able to keep up with the group. In the darkness, she and the child were separated from the rest of us. None of us noticed because we always kept moving. When we finally stopped and saw that she was not with us, none of us had the energy or the willpower to go looking for her.

We never saw or heard from her again. My best guess is that she and her baby died on the side of the mountain—and I feared that the same fate awaited me.

Even though I had strongly believed that my idea of "self" had been duly put to death in the Rite of Chod, I now realized how intense my aversion to real death really was. I desperately wanted to live. I knew that, in the teachings of Buddha, death was all a part of the natural cycle of birth, life, and death, but something instinctive in me kicked in that went beyond my intellect. My philosophy about the joys of death and rebirth went right out the window. The idea of death—real death—rained down on me a feeling of terror that I had never experienced before.

The next night, when everyone else stood up and readied themselves to walk into the endless black void of night, I stayed seated. I was not able to do any more.

My feet were in excruciating pain. Over and over again, they had been sliced and banged by the ice-cold, jagged rocks underfoot. The night temperature had dropped to freezing levels, and I had neither shoes nor insulated clothing. I was weak. I was cold. I was hungry. And I wanted to go back home.

"I can't go on any longer," I said to Joha. "Take me to the nearest village or take me back home. I can't go on any longer. I will die out here on these mountains if we do not find a nearby village where we can get help."

"We can't stop. You can't go back. Everyone here has paid me to take them to Nepal. No one has paid me to take them back."

I started to cry uncontrollably. My entire body trembled. "Please take me back. I don't want to die out here." I fell over onto my side, crying.

"Please." I was begging Joha to have mercy on me.

"Stand up! We must keep moving. You cannot stay here." Joha and another monk who was traveling with us came over, put their hands under my arms, and lifted me up. "You can't stay here. You have to keep moving. We do not have much further to go."

We do not have much further to go. I had heard him say that many times. I no longer knew what that meant, because even a step more seemed too far.

Reluctantly, I started to walk again on my own. I sobbed with every step, deeply regretting having left Lhasa.

We had walked for a little over an hour when I heard Joha tell me to stop. "Shhh," his voice came through the dark. "You hear that?"

I paused for a moment, and then, through the silence of the night, came the sound of rushing water.

"This is as far as we are going tonight. Rest here, and we will pick up tomorrow morning," Joha said.

The next morning, I awoke to one of the most amazing displays of natural scenery that I had ever seen in my life. Water was gushing out over a rocky ridge on the adjacent mountain across the valley where we were resting. The fluffy white mist plunged down the face of the mountain and dove into a crystal-blue serenity pool below. The mighty water roared and drowned out the voices of the people whom I could see standing in the valley.

I was captured in the moment.

Pointing off into the distance, Joha said, "Just over on the other side of that mountain is the border of Nepal. There you will wait for a bus that will take you to India. Welcome to Nyalam."

29
INDIA

I gazed through the window of the dirty, white bus, happy to start back on the road again after a month in Katmandu, Nepal. Even after my experience on the mountains, I felt a bit addicted to the restlessness of travel. Travel was a form of escape from the cage of dusty, stale teachings. The onslaught of these new experiences was slowly chipping away at the things that I thought I knew.

Just a year ago, I had thought I knew what physical pain was. The Himalayan mountains had taught me that I hadn't had a clue. I used to think that I knew what it was like to be cold. The mountain pass between Tibet and Nepal gave the word *cold* new meaning.

I seemed to be further away from being a lama than I had been a year before. My travels had taught me how little I knew and how little my faith was. Unable to hide behind my crimson robes, real fear and lack of faith had surged to the surface and revealed a shell of belief that was hollower than I had thought.

The long white bus shifted in the ruts along the dusty road as we pulled out of the bus station. The view from my seat was my window to a strange world that I was ready to leave behind. It was time now to continue on to India. My body had mostly recovered from the treacherous journey from Tibet. My feet were not completely healed, but I did not have enough money to stay in Nepal for long. Although my feet were still in pain, they were much better than when I had first arrived.

I might have liked to have stayed longer, but the people in Nepal were not as generous in their giving of alms to the monks as they were in Tibet. Besides that, the Nepalese police were not on the side of the Tibetans and were always on the lookout for Tibetan refugees. If you were caught, they would arrest you, beat you, put you on a bus, and take you back to Tibet. I had heard many horror stories about Tibetan monks who had been captured in Nepal and returned to the hands of the Chinese authorities.

My impression of Nepal, especially at first glance, was that it seemed to be a really poor place and in need of immediate relief. The common people dressed very poorly. Their clothes were little more than tattered rags. Additionally, the clothing that the common monks wore was noticeably different from that of Tibetan monks. In Nepal, the monks often wore a single layer of gold robes. If you looked closely enough from the side, you could see their skin under their robe. Tibetans wear two layers with a shawl.

Although it had been an honor and a privilege to visit Nepal, because it is the birthplace of Buddha, I had felt out of place there. The Nepalese monks had so many different gods that I was not accustomed to praying to. Their gods were foreign to me. Monkeys ran everywhere in front of the temple dedicated to Lord Shiva. The city was loud, chaotic, and pungent. It was odd to think that Nepal had once been a small kingdom run by Buddha's family.

I was used to clean rivers running through the mountains, but the stench of burning bodies often filled the air in the middle of the city by the river. The Nepalese burned their dead, and the litter from the ceremony filled the river. The main river in Katmandu was cluttered with garbage and partially burned wooden planks that had once ferried burning flesh to the afterlife.

When the air of Katmandu was not filled with the stench of dead bodies burning, it was filled with the overpowering smell of garlic. The Nepalese love to put garlic in their food, and this made it very difficult for me to eat my meals. The Tibetan people do not enjoy garlic as much as the Nepalese do, so their food does not contain a lot of garlic. What we do like, however, is beef. In Tibet, we liked to eat beef raw, but in Nepal, it was illegal to kill cattle. In Tibet, we worshipped the Dalai Lama, but in Nepal, they worshipped the cow. Consequently, beef was never on the menu at the hostel where I stayed. They often served some sort of special curry and naan bread. The people in Nepal also used their hands when they ate, and I found that practice a bit disgusting. The only people who ate with their hands in Tibet were beggars. Monks would never eat with their hands. Our hands are considered very unclean and therefore not good to use for eating.

I had high hopes that things would be much better in India. Besides, according to my uncle in Lhasa, I had family members who lived in India that I had never met before. I was able to purchase a bus ticket that would take me across the border. From there, I would have to take a series of buses to get to a temple that was about eight hours north of India's capital, New Delhi. I did not have a proper ID or travel documents, but I had been coached by fellow travelers from Tibet on what to do, what to say, and when to go across the border.

I was very excited about going to India, with the thought of possibly being taught by the Dalai Lama and studying under him. As I sat on the bus, I couldn't help a feeling of excitement in knowing that I was somehow following in the footsteps of Buddha. There were aspects about my journey to India that reflected the Buddha's own journey.

Like Buddha, I was leaving Nepal and traveling to India looking for enlightenment—and what he found changed the world.

Buddha was a Hindu, and unlike other religious leaders, his divine revelations were realized in his lifetime. He did not have to die before people recognized who he was. Disciples followed him and devoted their lives to him until his death. Buddha traveled to India and discovered *Bodhi*, which means enlightenment or awakening. Bodhi is the road to Abhidharma. To obtain Bodhi, Buddha wandered along the holy Ganges River looking for spiritual teachers who would be able to lead him to enlightenment. After finding the best teachers in the world and learning all they had to teach him, Buddha realized that he had not found enlightenment, so he continued his journey. I, too, was on a search for teachers to lead me to enlightenment.

And, as with my journey, Buddha experienced extreme suffering. He ate nothing for days at a time except for one grain of wheat and one sesame seed until he was little more than a thin layer of skin clinging to his bones. Birds made nests in his matted hair, and layers of dust covered his dried-up body as he went months without bathing. He slept on a bed of nails that pricked through his thin skin.

Finally, Buddha found a place under a tree for meditation and sat completely still for forty-nine days without uttering a word, and it was there that he was truly awakened. That tree, known as the Bodhi Tree, is a place of pilgrimage for Buddhists around the world who seek enlightenment. Others realized how Buddha had been enlightened and wanted to be awakened, too, so they followed him, and he taught them the truth about Bodhi.

Like Buddha, I, too, was on a pilgrimage and wanted to realize Bodhi before I died.

I hoped to find it in India.

30
DHARAMSHALA

India was mind-numbing. It was an ocean of sounds, colors, foods, temples, and people.

It was difficult to tell how many cities the bus drove through on the way to my destination. Horns buzzed from whirring traffic that came from every direction. However, it didn't seem that there were too many places where we didn't sit in a traffic jam. The streets and sidewalks were filled with people wearing colorful, flowing sarees, exposed brown bellies, and bare feet. No two sarees looked the same.

It was impossible for me to understand what was happening around me. Nothing was taking place linearly. Everything seemed random and chaotic. Everyone seemed to be acutely poor and exceedingly wealthy at the same time; the two were intermingled. Contrasts rested on layers of contrasts. Yet there was an oddly arousing, exotic nature to the country that appealed to my spirit. I knew that I was in the right place.

India was the birthplace of both Hinduism and Buddhism—and the two were mostly indistinguishable from one another. India's gods were as numerous as the spicy cuisines available from the street vendors.

After the long bus journey, I arrived at Dharamsala. Dharamsala is a small town tucked away in the mountains of northwest India and is the capital of the Central Tibetan Administration. It functions as the center of operations for Tibet's exiled government, awaiting the day when Tibetans will obtain independence from China.

When I stepped down from the bus, I immediately heard a strange, yet familiar, sound. It was the gruff voice of a Tibetan Buddhist monk praying a long, drawn-out mantra. However, instead of being spoken in a temple, it was being broadcast over public speakers.

In China, the only things I ever heard broadcast over public speakers were either commands coming from the police or the Chinese national anthem. To hear the sweet sound of a smooth mantra made me feel like I was home.

Here, the temples were tightly packed together with small shopping stalls that lined the large, grey, brick roads. White scarves, Buddha statues, sheepskin jackets, incense holders, and prayer beads were sold at every stall.

"Registration for Tibetans over here," I heard a woman shout out at our bus. I looked up to see a couple of other passengers following her directions.

"Registration?" I asked.

"Registration for Tibetans over here," she said again in a mechanical voice.

I followed a few other young men who were obviously responding to her directions. After only a few hundred meters, I found myself standing in a line to register for free food and shelter! It was an amazing system. All I had to do was share with them my name and family information and declare that I was from Tibet, and I was immediately accepted as a member of the community.

It was a remarkable feeling to be accepted in a country that at first had felt so strange and foreign. Right away, I identified with the people and culture there. When I heard the people talking, I understood everything they were saying because they were speaking Tibetan. While Amdo Tibetan is my main language, I flowed in and out of the Kham and Central Tibetan that were being loosely spoken all around me. My ears had opened up. I was no longer in Nepal or traveling on a bus where gargling sounds of gibberish were being uttered all around me. They were speaking my language!

"Sign here to enroll in the Tibetan Transit School," a young man said in perfect Amdo Tibetan.

"What is that?"

"The Tibetan Transit School is for refugees to get a free education in Tibetan, English, and several other subjects. The school is without cost for refugees fleeing religious persecution from China."

"Fleeing? I am not running from China."

The young man cocked his head at me as if I had made a funny sound to a small puppy.

"It doesn't really matter if you are running from China or trying to get a visa to live with a movie star in America, the Tibetan Transit School can help Tibetans who are living in India without the proper papers. It is a five-year school that gives free lessons in computer courses, painting, and vocational skills that can help you get a job when you leave."

I smiled. "I do not need a job when I leave. I came here to find knowledge. I am a monk from a monastery in Lhasa. I want to study under the Dalai Lama and learn from the lamas who serve under him."

"Oh. Well. You should just follow one of the monks. They will take care of you."

I nodded and turned to walk away.

"Hey," he called out. When I turned around, he motioned with his hand for me to come back. "Come, friend, come."

The young man leaned forward and said softly, "Don't talk to any foreigners or locals in Chinese about where you come from and what you are doing here. Don't share about how you got here, who helped you, or what route you used. Nothing. Do not share anything with anybody. Big news stories help make money for foreigners, but they only make things more difficult for everyone here. Plus, there are agents from China living here looking to shut this place down. So stick with your own kind."

I didn't fully understand what he was talking about, but I nodded again as if I did. "If I go up to the monastery, do you think they would have a place for me to sleep?" I asked.

"Probably, but if not, just come back down here. We have plenty of open racks for you to sleep in at the transition center dorms. There are always plenty of places to sleep and eat around here if you are from Tibet."

I bowed slightly forward to say thank-you and turned to walk away. Then I saw a group of monks who had been walking together through the market and were making their way up to the monastery. I jogged to catch up with them and started to walk behind them. I knew that I could just follow them and get everything sorted out with the lamas later in the day.

As I walked with them, I looked up at the mountains and wondered which of the houses was the one where the Dalai Lama lived. I knew that Dharamsala was the place where he resided, but I didn't know which house or building. I didn't even know if he was currently in India. But in my mind, I could picture him up there in one of the buildings, praying and blessing people.

I was closer to the Dalai Lama than I had ever been in my life, and I could not wait to meet with him.

31

THIKSAY MONASTERY

Once the monks in Dharamsala learned that I was affiliated with the Gelug sect of Tibetan Buddhism, they asked me to join a group of monks who were riding in a small truck to a place called Thiksay, in the region of Ladakh. So, I found myself taken to Thiksay Monastery in the mountains a couple of hours north—closer to the border of China.

Thiksay Monastery is an almost exact replica of the Potala Palace in Lhasa. "Welcome to the mini-Potala Palace," I heard someone in the truck say when I first arrived at Thiksay. It sits atop a massive mountain and the buildings are arranged in ascending order of importance. From the bottom of the mountain, it looked as if big white blocks had given birth to other white blocks coming down the mountain. The monastery was at the top of a flight of stairs weaving through a maze of white structures and stupas, winding up the mountain. The main monastery was painted red, was twelve stories high, and had two main chambers.

One of the first things that jumped out at me was the massive, forty-five-foot Maitreya Buddha statue. Maitreya Buddha is the "messiah" version of Buddha who will reincarnate in the future seated in the lotus position. His face is bronze-gold in color, and on his head is the five-part crown representing the stages of Buddha.

Several hundred monks, most of whom had escaped from Tibet, worked and prayed at Thiksay monastery. This was an extraordinary place, exuding reflection.

"There is nothing more painful in the journey to knowledge than the fearful habit of doubt. Doubt as a result of fear separates people. Lack of trust is doubt, and that is a poison that disintegrates friendships and breaks up pleasant relations. It is a thorn that irritates and hurts. It is a sword that kills."

A visiting monk was integrating quotes of Buddha with his own experiences in a way that I had never heard before. It was a powerful way to relate to the words of Buddha.

There was a pleasant silence as we meditated on his words. There was no rush. It was better to hear fewer words with meaning over a long period of time than to listen to rapid babble over a short period of time. We needed time for them to marinate.

"Thousands of candles can be lit from a single candle, and the life of the candle will not be shortened by lighting others. Doubt does not decrease when shared. Likewise, happiness never decreases by being shared. Your flame will burn no longer and no shorter than the length of your wick. You must decide how you will spend your time. How will you spread your flame? Will you light candles of doubt or happiness?" Again, the visiting monk paused so that we could chew on his words for a few moments in solitude.

"God is all around, but you do not notice because you doubt. What you notice is your next meal, your next rest, your next worry, your next fear. Doubt never removes your focus from these things. You do not doubt your next meal. You merely hope it comes, and when it comes, you eat it. It is that simple. You do not have to doubt your next sleep. When you get tired enough, you lie down and the sleep simply comes to you. These things that you focus on will not even be remembered in a day or two, but they will distract you from what you have been seeking your entire life."

The teacher stopped speaking, his eyes rolled back in his head, and he went into a trance-like state. He started to shake violently and make utterances that I could not understand. Suddenly, while in this trance, his voice changed octaves. He stopped shaking and turned to me. His forehead darkened and his eyes lit up. "But what keeps you from finding enlightenment is Mara."

A hush fell over the room and my hair stood on end. Everyone knew Mara and feared him. Mara is the demon that attacked Buddha and tried to keep him from reaching enlightenment.

"Mara is sinking his fangs into your soul and fills you with the solid blackness of doubt. He spins a web of angry souls that surrounds you with misery and doubt. He is the agent of antagonism. He hurls passions, greed, and lust at you to obstruct your meditation. But can he hurt you?" the teacher asked. "Can Mara kill you?"

No one answered.

"Mara's fangs are long, his body is covered in the blood of his victims, and he holds the power of war and disease in his hand, but he is actually afraid of you. He fears your possible enlightenment. He fears that you will learn that he only has the power that you give him. Lokas like Mara are demons that are limited in the physical pain they can cause. Their torment can be cruel, but they can only cross the threshold of the spirit world if you give them the bridge. When you were born, there were lokas that were assigned to you. When your jiva, or life force of the soul, was given a body, hungry lokas began to follow you around. They waited patiently for the right time to leech onto you. They planted seeds of pain in your mind when you were only a baby, and they have worked to multiply their power over your life since that day."

As he spoke, I felt a cool breeze blowing in from the windows, but it did not feel like the natural wind. It felt spiritual.

"Your grief is like music to Mara, because your grief leads to the creation of bad karma. When you have bad karma long enough, you soon find it solidified in the finality of death. Yama, the lord of death, waits for you in the underworld and holds the keys for your jiva to pass from one world to the other. The lords of karma await to assign to you the next lifetime, which will go backward because of the bad karma that you carry. Your pain and misery are amplified and Mara is victorious."

"How can I defeat doubt?" I asked. "How can I defeat Mara?"

"You must become Mara. Instead of Mara living in you, you must live in Mara. Instead of you fearing Mara, Mara must fear you. Cast away all doubt. Cast away all fear. Walk among the gods of the underworld as if you belong. Become a loka to defeat the loka.

"The underworld must be as natural for you as the Pure Abodes, or the place reserved for those who have attained true enlightenment. Good does not exist without evil. Dark does not exist without light. Too often, as we try to obtain good, we attempt to destroy evil. Instead of obtaining good, you spend all of your energy trying to destroy that which cannot be destroyed. In the end, your efforts actually contribute to more growth of the very thing you try to destroy. Trying to gain faith by destroying doubt is impossible."

He paused for a moment and then continued, his voice returning to normal. "If you do not want to think about something and try hard to not think about it, does it help you think about it less? Stop fighting the opposite of what you want and realize that it is necessary to obtain what you desire. Embrace both the good and the bad and realize that they are both essential. Light and dark coexist. To reach one, you must accept the other, and when you finally attain what you are looking for, you will find that there was really no difference between the two anyway. After all, the real difference between any two ideas is only imagined."

A monk in a temple in northern India.

Monks studying in northern India.

Monks at a ceremony in India.

Monks debating at Sera Monastery in Tibet.

Chengdu, China.

A lotus flower.

Part Three:
Enlightened by Love and Sacrifice

32

A CHRISTIAN FAMILY MEMBER

"Tenzin!"

"Yes?" I responded to the unknown voice yelling down the corridor after me.

"There is someone outside looking for you."

I ended my meditation, stood up, and walked to the door. As I stepped outside, I saw a kind-looking young man, a little older than I, pacing around.

"Tenzin?" he said as soon as he saw me. I nodded.

"I'm Peema. Your uncle told me that you have been looking for us."

"Ahh…so good to see you. My uncle told me that I had family living here, but I didn't even know where to start. I was told that your family was living in Dharamsala. I asked around about you, but no one knew where you were."

"Yes, we used to live in Dharamsala, but we moved to America a year ago."

"I heard that you are a monk."

"I used to be, but not anymore."

I pulled my head back in surprise. "Not anymore? What happened? Did you decide you needed a wife?" I asked jokingly. Marriage was the number-one killer of monastic living.

"Not exactly," he said a bit sheepishly. "Do you care to take a walk?"

"Sure."

Peema and I strolled down the side of the mountain from the monastery. There wasn't really anywhere to walk to, but taking a walk in the shadow of the mountains and away from the listening ears of other monks seemed to be what my relative wanted to do.

"My family is living in America and they really like it a lot. America is nothing like Tibet or India. Everything there is so much better. Everyone has a car, a house, and a mobile phone."

"How did you get to go to America?" I asked.

"We were invited by a Christian man. Their church sponsored our visa and have helped us."

"Christian?" I had heard the word before. I knew that it was the religion of Westerners but didn't know anything about it.

"Yes. There was an American who came to Dharamsala and told us about Jesus. We listened to him, and what he had to say changed our lives forever. We have never been happier, and we are doing better than any generation before us."

I was shocked at what he was saying. Although I didn't know much about the religion of the Christians, I did know that Tibetans hated their religion. Even Hindus, who recognize almost every god under the sun, hate Christians.

I had heard about Christians sneaking around like snakes and trying to trick Tibetans to believe their religion. Once you accept their religion, you become their slave and have to do what they tell you to do.

"Did the Americans trick you?" I asked, feeling sorry for him. "Do you need help to escape?"

"What? No! I live in America, not China. You do not need to escape from America. You can leave whenever you like. They do not have guards keeping you in. It is not like China where there are guards making sure that people do not escape. Instead, in America, they have guards trying to keep the people out because so many people want to go there."

"You mean like India?"

"Not exactly. America is much better than India. I lived in Dharamsala for many years, but I never really felt at home. I was always considered to be a refugee from my homeland of Tibet. The longer I lived in Dharamsala, the more I hated it."

"Yes, but they give you so many things for free. Isn't that what everyone wants?"

"Not when the free stuff is barely scraps and there is no avenue to make yourself better. I couldn't get hired at a better job to provide more money for my family. I couldn't move us out of Dharamsala on my own. India would never allow me to move to New Delhi and get a job or open a small shop or be the boss of my own business. Then, when the American came around, he told me about Jesus and how Jesus gives us hope for the future. He gave me a book about the life of Jesus, and the stories were unlike anything I had ever read."

"Peema," I interrupted. "Do you need my help for something?"

"No. I came here for you, not for me. Your uncle told me that you were here all alone and didn't know anyone and might need some help. God has put you on my heart. I have been waking up late at night thinking of you and praying for you—even though I have never met you before. I have been thinking about you even in my dreams. I traveled all the way up here in obedience to God."

"In your dreams?"

"Yes. Dreams were a powerful channel for Jesus to communicate with me before I knew who He was. At first, I thought Jesus was a divine daka who bypassed my physical mind to communicate directly with my spirit through dreams, but He is so much more than that. Jesus brought a light to my life, and He can do the same for you."

Peema was crossing the line. He was doing something that was extremely dangerous at the monastery. If the other monks knew what he was talking about, they would beat him to a bloody pulp. "I am sorry, Peema. I do not know if I want to hear anymore. I think…I think I must go."

"Wait. I am staying here tonight. I would like to talk more tomorrow. After tomorrow, I will return to America."

"I don't know. I do not think the lamas would appreciate what you are saying."

"What am I saying?" Peema challenged.

"Look, I do not want to debate you, I just—"

"You do not want to debate me? Are you not Tibetan? I thought debate was how we learned what is true and what is not true."

I did not respond. I did not want anything bad to happen to Peema, and I knew that his life would be short-lived if the others knew what he was doing.

"Goodbye, Peema."

"Will I see you tomorrow?" he asked.

I didn't answer him. I just wished him blessings and walked back up to the monastery. I didn't tell anyone there about my conversation with Peema. I hoped that I would quickly forget about it and that he could go back and live the rest of his life in America.

33

"MORE DEADLY THAN MARA"

After my meeting with Peema, it was hard for me to sleep that night. I went walking through the empty rooms of the meditation chambers. The echo of my feet shuffling across the floor bounced off of the dark walls. I didn't know anything about Peema's new religion, but something in me rejected it.

Yet I also felt tormented by my automatic rejection of his new belief. It irritated me to the core and I could not rationalize it in my mind. His words kept coming back to me over and over again: "You do not want to debate me? Are you not Tibetan? I thought debate was how we learned what is true and what is not true."

"Troubled minds can't find rest," came a voice from one of the corners. It was the voice of our visiting monk.

"Sorry, I didn't know anyone was awake."

"I am still on American time," he said.

"You live in America?"

"Uhhmmm," he said with a nod. "I am getting too old for this travel back and forth."

"Have you lived in America long?" I asked.

"More than forty years."

"Have you ever met any Christians during your time in America?"

Silence.

"Have *you* ever met any Christians?" he finally responded after a time of pondering my question.

"I have, Teacher. I have met one."

"What did this Christian say to you?"

"He did not say much. He just told me that the name of their God is Jesus and He can visit us in dreams."

Again there was silence.

"Did he say anything more about Jesus to you?"

"No."

"Does that person live here among us?"

"No," I said, instinctively knowing that I somehow needed to protect Peema's identity.

"Never speak to the Christians. They will suck the prana, the energy source that flows through all living things, from your soul. In Tibet, prana flows like streams of living water over the mountains and saturates every living being with internal channels of power. Prana is the life force of the body and the wind in the mind found in all living creatures. Prana carries us from origin to our destination. Prana gives us breath from karma to karma. Prana allows us to visit loka in the underworld or obtain the advice of the gods. Those who harness the power of prana are able to levitate, fly, or do other superhuman acts.

"Prana isn't just a power that gives life—it is the breath of life. It feeds off of our mantras. It grows from our prayers. It has its foundation in the reading aloud of holy texts. As your master, I pass on my prana to you and you pass it on to others, but Christians have a mystical power source that interrupts the flow of prana. Christians take away your power and strip you of your prana. Stay away from them and do not listen to their words."

"Couldn't we expose the fallacy with a simple debate?"

The teacher's head whipped around, and he glared at me. "Do not play with Jesus, boy! He is more deadly than Mara and will keep you from enlightenment. Mara only has the power to trick you out of your prana, but Jesus can take it away. Mara can conquer you with darkness, but Jesus will conquer you with light. Unlike Mara, Jesus can control the life force of your jiva. I have seen it. I have seen the power of those who follow Jesus."

Chills shivered down my spine at the thought of a force more intimidating than Mara.

"Jesus and his followers destroy the entire order of all that we know," he continued.

"How?" I asked.

He puffed at me as if my question annoyed him. He seemed a bit miffed that I didn't know exactly what he was talking about, but I didn't. I honestly didn't know how one god—one that I had never heard of—could disrupt the entire order of heaven and earth.

"The loka of the underworld do not trifle with Jesus. We should not even be discussing him. Talking about him gives him power. He disrupts the entire order of all that we know, because he can overpower the loka of the underworld and the gods that lead us to enlightenment. He destroys the Middle Way. Even Yama, the lord of death, leaves him alone, because Jesus would release the spirits from their bondage and turn them loose! If a spirit escapes the bondage of Yama before their time to be released, they can go in between the different realms and wreak havoc on us all."

I was dumbfounded at what he was telling me.

"If Jesus is so dangerous, Teacher, why have I never heard about him before? Wouldn't it be better to warn others about his danger so that we can better prepare against him?"

The teacher laughed. "You don't prevent the spread of a virus by bringing it to your home and evaluating it. You keep it as far from you and your family as possible. And you don't bring Jesus to your temple to evaluate his dangers! You keep his name as far from your students as possible. You lock him out. Unlike the other gods, Jesus is given power through sharing about him. He is like a deadly virus—by the time you realize how deadly he is, he has already infected everyone in your home.

"Why did you come here?" he asked.

"I came here to find the ultimate dharma—to find enlightenment."

"If dharma is what you seek, then you must cleanse your mind of everything that you have heard about Jesus. No matter how little of a place you give him, he can use it to destroy everything—just as a virus that you cannot see with your naked eye has the power to destroy the health of a well, strong body.

"Stay away," he said again with emphasis. "Stay far, far away."

I bowed in the darkness, acknowledging his command to me.

As I walked away, he added, "Do not tell anyone here about our conversation. You must contain this virus or else...."

"Remember, this very temple that gives you shelter was built as a reflection of perfect order," he said, referring to the name *Thiksay*, which means "perfect order." "You will destroy that perfect order for eternity if Jesus is allowed to infect the minds of those who have come here to find enlightenment."

I bowed again and walked away toward my room, running my fingers over the smooth edges of my prayer beads and praying for strength and wisdom.

I couldn't help but think of Peema and his words to me. He and his family must have known about the dangers of Jesus. Why had he considered it so important to tell me about something so dangerous? Peema didn't look like he had been suffering from any pain or spiritual torment. In fact, he looked and acted as if he had a peace and calmness to him.

After I returned to my room, I was still unable to sleep. There were so many questions running through my mind. I wanted to know more about Jesus. I think that my newly found desire to learn more sprang from the fact that I now knew I was not supposed to know anything about him!

My curiosity was itching, and now I wanted nothing more than to scratch it.

34

TEACHINGS OF THE DALAI LAMA

There was excitement in the air. Everyone was preparing for the arrival of the Dalai Lama. His Holiness was riding in an entourage from his residence near Dharamsala to Thiksay Monastery. We knew that he would not arrive too early, because he would be stopping in Shey Village to pray at a holy site.

The head lama, Thiksay Rinpoche, was preparing to receive him. A grand room decorated in crimson and gold was set up for him in which to teach and pray. A golden throne was placed at the head of the room and centered so that it would be the most commanding location for the Dalai Lama to speak from.

His Holiness would be speaking and teaching beside Thiksay Rinpoche, who was greatly revered as one of the top lamas in the world. He had studied at the Drepung Monastery in Tibet until his escape from the Chinese.

Looking out from the monastery, I could see a long line of dedicated followers starting to make their trek up the mountain. Monks and nuns from all traditions, public officials, and pilgrims, along with schoolchildren from the nearby small town of Leh, were making their way to the temple. They were all hoping to catch a glimpse of the Dalai Lama and to hear his wise teachings.

I watched the crowds to see if I could spot Peema among them. I hadn't gone out to see him the day after I met him, but I found myself thinking about him often—more often than I wanted to. I assumed he had flown back to America and I would never see him again. I didn't know if that made me happy or sad.

Suddenly, I heard chanting in the grand teaching hall. That was the signal it was about time for us all to begin prayer and prepare for the arrival of the Dalai Lama. I had waited for this moment for my entire life, but it didn't feel as special as I'd thought it would.

I looked down the mountain and saw a convoy of vehicles roaring down the road toward our mountain and knew that it must be His Holiness. The pilgrims at the bottom of the mountain began to wave and cheer with excitement. Some of them ran after the vehicle. I quickly made my way to the great teaching hall before the temple got so crowded with people that it would be hard to get there.

I sat in a praying position and waited. After some time, I could tell that the Dalai Lama was getting closer because the decibel level of people's voices outside was growing. And then, he walked into the room. His big, round-rimmed eyeglasses covered half of his face, and his smile lit up the place. Light from the sun glowed on the top of his bald head. His crimson and gold robe flowed flawlessly to the floor and oddly matched the heavy drapes in the room. He hunched a bit forward in a humble bowing motion as he slowly walked toward the podium.

A pack of journalists and photographers documented his every move. Camera shutters rapidly clicked in machine-gun fashion. Most of these journalists did not look Tibetan or Indian. They were white foreigners, and they were wearing clothing that did not fit in at the temple at all.

The Dalai Lama stood behind the podium and steadied himself. Thiksay Rinpoche and His Holiness prayed an auspicious prayer and then the Dalai Lama began to speak. A thin, barely noticeable, wireless microphone reached around his cheek and made a popping sound whenever he said something with emphasis.

He began by stating that, as human beings, we are all fundamentally the same. Instead of focusing on our similarities, we often focus on our differences, such as race, religion, or economic status.

"As I travel the world and meet people, I always consider myself just one of the seven billion human beings alive today. I don't think of myself as a Tibetan or a Buddhist or even as the Dalai Lama. I have lots of friends because I treat everyone equally as another human being."

He said that he was greatly saddened by the conflicts that were the result of our differences in religion. "All religions teach love, compassion, forgiveness, and tolerance, so there is no basis for conflict between them."

I leaned forward, eagerly drinking in every single word. It was no wonder that he was so famous. His words flowed effortlessly, like poetry, and not one of them was wasted on vanity. Each sentence he spoke was as equally profound as the one before it, and his teaching was exactly what I needed.

It was almost as if he were reading my mind. After hearing about the religion that followed Jesus, it was good to hear that the Dalai Lama did not seem to be as aggressive against his teachings as was the visiting teacher who had come several months earlier on the day I had met with Peema.

"Here in Ladakh, I am happy to see that Buddhists and Muslims have good relations and live together in peace and harmony. This is something very precious about Ladakh that you must preserve. It's a treasure that others in India and the world at large may admire."

The Dalai Lama pointed to us and said that we must show love to every man, no matter what his race, religion, or financial status. There was delayed clapping at the back of the room from the foreigners who had just heard the translation of what the Dalai Lama had said.

Then, it seemed as if the Dalai Lama was looking straight at me when he said it was our choice to be Buddhists or not, but if we chose to be Buddhists, then we must be twenty-first century Buddhists. He told us that we could not lean on blind faith but must study hard and use logic and debate as the primary tools to gain understanding. He challenged us not to be narrow-minded, but instead to open our minds to all manner of thought and to learn from our fellow man.

My mind jumped with excitement. The heavy burden that I had felt from thinking about the dangers of Jesus rolled off my shoulders when he said that we should be open to other faiths and respect them.

After he finished speaking, we all went to lunch, and after lunch, the Dalai Lama returned to answer some of our questions. One of the students from Leh asked the Dalai Lama how we could achieve peace when there was so much violence in the world. The Dalai Lama responded by reiterating that we see the conflict because we focus too strongly on the things that divide us instead of the things that unite us. He again pointed out that the

Hindus, Muslims, and Buddhists all live in Leh and respect one another—living in peace and harmony.

It seemed that the Dalai Lama had repeated that line several times during the day, but only when he said it to the student who asked the question did I realize that he had not said anything about Jesus. Suddenly, my enthusiasm was curbed.

"Why is he leaving out the followers of Jesus when he speaks of living in peace and harmony?" I thought to myself. "Was the teacher right when he said that we should not even mention the name of Jesus? Did the Dalai Lama fear to bring up the name of Jesus when listing the different religions that are able to live in harmony with one another?"

And just like that, as fast as I had felt relieved and unshackled, I found myself once again strapped with the torment of thinking about Jesus.

35
THE SIGN OF THE CROOKED CROSS

After several years of living and studying at the Thiksay Monastery, I had settled into a routine. Most of the time, I felt bored with reading and meditating. I longed for a different kind of mental stimulation.

The stimulation I longed for was information outside of the Buddhist texts. I had access to a library of Buddhist writings filled with stories, chants, and mantras, but I didn't have access to information about other religions. I didn't know the difference between a Sunni and a Shia Muslim—although I had heard the Dalai Lama talk about them.

There was so much about how the world worked that I didn't know. I didn't know how a car was put together, how airplanes were able to fly, or how rivers could flow to the sea but never run dry. Likewise, there were so many things around me that didn't make sense, and there was a part of me that felt I was learning a lot about nothing at the monastery. I longed to know more.

I hadn't known anything about Nepal, other than what I had learned from the stories of Buddha, until I traveled there for the first time. I hadn't known anything about Indian language or culture until I took a bus to India. Perhaps I needed firsthand knowledge of those other aspects of life, so I could learn about them, too.

Not least of all, I wanted to know why my family members had fled to America and why Americans sought enlightenment from Jesus instead of Buddha.

I had not been getting much sleep, and I was exhausted. I spent most days walking around like a zombie and spent most nights awake and alone. Without anything new to stimulate my mind, I found myself sleeping during the day. There was a strict policy against this, but I had become an expert at finding hiding places where I could sleep without anyone knowing. There were so many new monks coming and going from the monastery that no one really noticed when I was not around.

One day, the monks were all gathered on the side of the mountain, divided into groups of two to debate for the entire morning. Debates were one of the few times during the week that I participated in a mental activity that gave me life. I had been placed in charge of several new monks to teach them and train them, but regurgitating old stories was no longer exciting for me. Reading the same story for the millionth time was so mechanical that it required no brain power.

For that morning's debate, I had been paired with a new monk who had just arrived from Tibet only a few weeks ago. It was my job to bring him under my wing and teach him. I asked the new student to be seated and to be prepared to be challenged. I could tell that he was nervous. He took a seated position and began praying to prepare for the debate. I shared with him the same advice that Tashi Lama had given me years before: "Don't try to look for your mistakes when you debate. Mistakes give birth to the blindness to your own folly. Look for seeds in the questions and give birth to truth through those seeds. Fear will pull you onto one of two paths— one is to freeze and the other is to panic. Look for the middle path between freezing and panic. There you will find your footing."

The young man nodded.

"Om a ra pa ca na dhih." I began to pray to appeal to the Buddha of wisdom to start the debate.

"The Right-coiled White Conch is just one of the Eight Auspicious Symbols that makes the sounds of dharma teachings and awakens us from our deep slumber of ignorance," I said with a pounding clap.

I started off with elementary Buddhism. The Eight Auspicious Symbols were taught in every children's classroom near the monastery. Even the youngest of students knew them.

"The Precious Umbrella symbolizes our preservation under the three lower realms when the rains of doubt come. When the rains of doubt fill the waters of the realms, we do not drown. Instead we find the Golden Fish—the symbol of our ability to adapt to the floods and swim freely in the teachings of Buddha."

I smacked my hands together and faced the young monk seated on the ground to see if he was following me.

"I accept," he replied.

One by one, I went through four of the five remaining elements of the Eight Auspicious Symbols: the Dharma Wheel, Lotus Flower, Holy Vase, and Endless Knot.

"What of the Victory Banner—our symbol of military victory over the elements of pride, desire, emotions, and death? The Victory Banner can also be said to be our victory of Buddhist doctrine over other teachings," I continued, smacking my hands together.

"I accept," he said again like a good, compliant new monk.

"And what of the supreme auspicious symbol that is not a part of the Eight Auspicious Symbols but can be found everywhere, on every continent, throughout the history of man—the Swastika?" The Swastika, or Manji, tainted in many Westerners' minds because of its association with Nazi Germany, is one of the most-used, auspicious symbols and is found everywhere in Tibet. It is a crooked cross that can either have positive energy or negative energy, depending on its direction.

"Swastika means 'well-being' or 'it is,' but another ancient meaning for the word is 'ultimate victory.' Unlike all other auspicious signs, a Swastika is a sign that helps us remember that we have ultimate victory in our Buddhist thoughts and teachings."

"I accept," came the response again.

As the debate continued, I became more excited. I could feel my intellect becoming engaged and the essence of the debate taking on real meaning. I came to a place where I felt there was no right and wrong—only exploration. To turn right or left did not matter. The truth was all one big room to be explored, and which side I explored first did not matter.

"If I have ultimate victory and the Swastika is my banner of ultimate victory, then what have we to fear from the teachings of other religions? We could absorb them and, over time, their falsehood would eventually die out. Under our banner of ultimate victory, we could invite the Muslims to join us at the temple and learn from our ways and we learn from their ways in the same way the Buddha learned from the Hindus and the Hindus learned from him. The things that they believe would be challenged by the things that we believe, and in open and honest debate, we would see clearly to the right path."

The young monk sat speechless. His eyes shifted from side to side to see if anyone else was listening to what I was saying. I didn't care. I was not actually talking to him any longer. I was have an open discussion with myself.

"Ultimate victory is not just a symbol found in the Swastika, but it is a virtue of truth, and the sign is simply a reminder from the gods. When the rains of doubt are heavy, we find shelter under our Precious Umbrella. When the floodwaters fill the earth, we are like the Golden Fish that swim underwater naturally. When the end of the day comes, the Victory Banner is flown as a symbol to the spirit world that Buddha overcame the obstacles between him and enlightenment. It was a long battle, but he overcame."

The other debates were already wrapping up, and I could tell that our time was up, but I ended feeling that I wanted to know more about those who followed Jesus. I was not sure how I could do that or when I could start, but the Swastika was a reminder that I did not need to be afraid of what I would learn.

36
WHAT SEVEN YEARS IN INDIA TAUGHT ME

"Tenzin!" I heard someone shout my name. "You have a letter!"

I had not had a letter from home since my arrival at the Thiksay Monastery seven years earlier. After I was handed the letter, I immediately opened it. The message was a very simple one written by my oldest brother.

Tenzin,

I have bad news about our father. Two tribes near our village were fighting with one another, and because of their respect for our father, he traveled to the village to mediate their dispute.

The mediation went well and everyone celebrated with a special banquet dinner. After the dinner, our father became deathly ill from food poisoning. We wanted to take him to a hospital, but it was too far away.

I am sorry to write to tell you that he did not make it. Our father has died.

Please come back home for the funeral and to see mother.

I didn't read further. Crushing pain and anguish immediately rushed over me.

"My father is dead," I said out loud.

Suddenly, in the flash of a moment, the meaning of death changed for me. All of the teachings and writings that I had learned, recited, and taught to others gave me no comfort at all. I folded the letter and started to silently sob.

An empty void that I didn't know existed was now all I could think about. I had been living in India for the last seven years and earnestly seeking enlightenment. It had never occurred to me even one time that the day would come when my family members would pass away and I would forever lose the chance to see them again.

I didn't have any photos of my father. Living a monastic life, I owned nothing and had come to India with nothing. The only images I had of my father were the ones I carried in my memory. I tried to close my eyes and imagine his face, but it was difficult. The truth is that those memories were from so long ago that they were rather hazy—almost nonexistent. I could conjure a fuzzy image of him, but the details of his face escaped me. I had forgotten exactly what he looked like.

Any chance of making a new memory with my father, seeing his face one last time, and telling him all the things that I wanted to say to him was now gone forever. My belief in life after death gave me no comfort. There was still a finality to it all, and that made the pain of his passing even greater.

In the seven years that I had been at the monastery, I had sat and listened to the Dalai Lama teach about death and reincarnation over and over again, for hours at a time. The Dalai Lama himself was proof of reincarnation. I enjoyed every one of his visits and was even able to join in small conversations with him and pose simple questions, but now his wise words did not comfort me in the least.

One of the senior monks of the monastery noticed my sobbing. "What happened?" he asked with genuine concern.

"I got a letter from my brother. It seems that my father has passed."

He didn't respond.

"I have to return home," I said.

"At least there is comfort in the order."

"What do you mean?"

"A father being buried by his son is natural. The son will then be buried by his son and so on and so on. There is no doubt that it is painful, but imagine the far greater pain that accompanies the father who must bury his son. It is not the natural order of things for a father to have to bury his son." He paused. "We monks can take comfort in the order."

"Is the order the same for us?" I snapped. "My father and mother are the closest family that I will ever have in this world. Unlike the lamas and even the Dalai Lama—I will never know what it is like to have a family."

The monk looked at me as if I had said something untrue.

"What? Come on," I continued. "You know what I am talking about. Almost all of these leaders have wives and families outside of the monastery whom they sneak away and see when no one is looking. The Dalai Lama himself has several."

"You are speaking from pain."

"Are you honestly going to stand there and tell me that the Dalai Lama is celibate like you and me?"

He smiled. He knew that the jig was up. It was not a subject that any of us liked to acknowledge, but the most senior monks knew that the senior lamas, including the Dalai Lama, had secret relationships that were hidden from the outside world.

"My family lineage only goes up and sideways—that's it! Because of the oath that I have taken, it will not continue through me. In a strange way, my father is my legacy. I am not his."

I turned and walked toward my room before I said anything more. I had already said enough to worry the senior monks at the monastery if they ever heard what I was openly talking about.

After I returned to my room, I began to gather my things. I smiled through my tears as I thought about the funny things that my father used to say when I was young. All of the harsh things that he said were suddenly difficult to remember.

My emotions continued to switch back and forth between grief and nostalgia, the two coming in waves. Both emotions also brought with them a strong sense of doubt about my entire faith. I was left wondering if my Buddhist faith had any truth to it at all. Thoughts about Jesus kept coming to my mind. I longed to know more about these followers of Jesus and what they thought about death and the afterlife. Yet, although I was full of doubts and questions, these were being partially suppressed by my new objective—returning to China.

It was time to go back home. I desperately wanted to see my mother and my siblings. I wanted nothing more.

The death of my father made me reflect on the things I had learned at Thiksay Monastery. I had traveled to India seeking enlightenment, and looking back over the past seven years, I realized that what those years had really taught me was to love and appreciate my family members while I still had them.

Sadly, it had taken the death of my father to teach me about the need to live life with those whom we love. Ironically, in the deepest part of my sadness, I finally felt enlightened.

37
BACK TO TIBET

I had saved up over eight thousand Chinese yuan during my time at Thiksay Monastery. Thiksay was a relatively wealthy monastery because of all the foreign endowments and donations given for the refugee Tibetan monks, and every month, we were given money for various things.

Eight thousand Chinese yuan is considered a lot of money in my village and would make me a rather wealthy monk back in China. It would be enough to build a home outside of the monastery if I so desired. However, returning to China was dangerous because I still did not have the proper travel papers. I knew that the chances of going back by bus with no problems would be risky—but I also remembered all too clearly the trip that I had made to Nepal through the Himalayan mountains and did not want to relive even one part of that horrible adventure.

I was able to take the bus from India to Nepal with no problems. The officials at the border were used to processing Tibetan monks and gave me as little hassle as possible for traveling without a passport. However, when I arrived at the Nepal-China border, the immigration officer asked me to step into a back room, where they demanded to see my travel documents. When I failed to produce anything, they told me to place my hands behind my back, and they put me in handcuffs.

I sat handcuffed for a couple of hours in the back room until an officer came and shouted something at me in the Nepali language. They told me to get into the back of their police truck, and then they drove me to the border. From the Nepalese side, I could see two big, red Chinese flags on either side of the road. Guards in green uniforms waved the truck through.

When the vehicle stopped, its back gate was opened and I was told to get out. Two Chinese guards came from behind me and grabbed my arms. They almost lifted me off the ground as they brought me to the immigration building.

I should have been scared, but I wasn't. Deep down, I had known this would be the price I would pay if I didn't take the mountain route by foot again. I knew that at some point or another, I would have to be punished for leaving Tibet without permission if I ever wanted to return home again.

The fact that I hadn't even bothered to change into civilian clothes did not help things either. Yet the decision to leave my crimson robes on instead of wearing jeans and a jacket was one that I willingly made. My Tibetan monk robes had advantages and disadvantages. In India and Nepal, my robes had granted me special treatment. Most times, my fellow passengers on buses had given me free food. The bus drivers had often given me a preferable front seat with the hope that treating me nicely would benefit their level of karma. The Indian immigration officers had waved me through their lines with few questions.

However, all of the special benefits stopped at the Chinese border. The Chinese border guards did not see me as a peaceful monk. They saw me as an antirevolutionary rebel. To them, I was someone who represented Tibetan independence. They knew that monks like me traveled to India for only one reason—to train with the Dalai Lama and coordinate with the exiled Lhasa government.

The guards placed me in a holding cell where I stayed overnight. The next day, they put me into a vehicle and told me they were driving me to Lhasa. In Lhasa, I was taken to the police station and put into solitary confinement. I asked for water, but they did not even acknowledge that I had spoken. I had not had anything to eat or drink in almost two days. I started to yell from behind the bars, begging anyone who could hear me for a drink of water, but there was no response. I called out until I had no energy left and fell asleep.

I was abruptly awakened by water being splashed on my face. "Here is your water!" shouted one of the prison guards. "Get up!"

I looked up and saw three guards and a man in black clothing standing over me in my cell. The night had crept in while I was sleeping and it was not easy to see their faces. When I tried to stand, one of the guards kicked me in the chest and knocked me back down.

The man wearing all black yelled something at me, but I could not make it out. He was speaking too fast; my facility in Mandarin Chinese was not good enough to allow me to follow along. It seemed that one of the guards had asked me something, but I hadn't responded because I hadn't understood, so he kicked me in the thigh. "You better answer me!" he finally yelled.

"Ting bu dong! Ting bu dong!" I yelled out. This means "I do not understand" in Chinese.

"My name is Mr. Wang," the man in black said very slowly. "Now, tell me. Where did you go in India? Where did you live?"

"I only traveled to see my family."

"Liar! You are working for the Dalai Lama," Mr. Wang replied.

"No, I do not work for the Dalai Lama."

"Did you see the Dalai Lama? Did you meet with him while you were in India?"

One of the guards grabbed my hair and lifted my head up to face Mr. Wang. "Did you meet with the Dalai Lama?" he asked again.

"I only saw him a few times, but he never noticed me. I am too lowly for him."

"Liar," Mr. Wang said again. One of the other guards hit me in the face. My mouth went numb for a moment and then I tasted blood.

Mr. Wang said something about my working to overthrow the Chinese government, but I couldn't fully understand what he was saying. "Why have you returned to China?" he demanded to know.

"I have returned to China because my father died."

"Where is your family in India?"

"They no longer live in India. They are now living in America. My only family is here in Tibet."

Bam! One of the guards hit me again. "Tibet is China," he yelled. "You are Chinese. Your family lives in China!"

Mr. Wang and the guards who were with him questioned me for what seemed like an unbearably long time, and then they transferred me to another jail cell before daybreak.

I was kept in a cell with two other men for six months, and then I was finally released to go and see my family.

38
A TIBETAN FUNERAL

I made my way by bus to the mountains of my childhood in Jichu, where I lived with my mother for the next month. Family members and neighbors stopped by every day, along with the monks from the monastery. The monks often brought food and words of comfort.

I was surprised when I saw that one of my older brothers had become a monk at the local monastery. Soon after my two eldest brothers had found wives and settled down, my other brother, Duuka, decided he wanted to follow in my footsteps.

When I had left for India to study under the Dalai Lama, my mother and father told everyone about it, so I had become a bit of a hometown hero. Not many people from Jichu have had the opportunity to go and study under the very person whose picture they have hanging in their homes. However, my newfound fame did not take away the sting of having missed the final years of being with my father. And I had also missed his funeral.

Participating in a relative's funeral is very important in Buddhism to help fight for their spirit. The cycle of the soul takes a total of seven weeks after death. Family members pray intensely over deceased family members for forty-nine days because that is the time when the spirit is in between heaven and earth, and demons and gods come to make their claims. People offer these fervent prayers so that the spirit of their family member will not be snatched by a demon and dragged to the lower realms.

My father was honored in a traditional Celestial funeral ceremony. Celestial funerals are a Tibetan practice that go back a thousand years. With this type of burial, the spirit of a person is expected to reach heaven more quickly. After my father died, he was wrapped in white, Tibetan cloth and prayed over by local monks for three days. Holy scriptures were read over the body to allow a peaceful transition for the spirit. My brother was one of the monks who prayed over my father and read scriptures.

After three days, his body was arranged in a fetal position, placed in a bag that looked similar to a backpack, and carried up a mountain to the Celestial burial platform, which is a large, flat rock elevated above the other mountains.

Several monks waited for him, chanting mantras and burning incense. Their prayers and chanting recognized the transmigration of the spirit without the body. The body is merely an empty vessel when the spirit leaves it.

A special butcher, known as a body-breaker, was brought up to the ceremonial rock. My father was spread out on the rock facedown, and the body-breaker methodically fileted the flesh from his back and head. His body was then laid out in pieces and fed to large vultures. Vultures are considered to be holy birds for the Celestial ceremonial burial because they do not prey upon other birds but instead focus on the offering. If the birds eat everything, it is considered to be a successful ceremony. If the birds leave any part of the body uneaten, then it is considered to be a sign of bad energy that is not holy enough for the birds to eat. I was told that the birds left nothing behind and my father had been carried into the heavens that day.

While a Celestial funeral is the most customary way for Tibetan commoners to say goodbye to their loved ones, it is also one of the most controversial. During the Cultural Revolution in China, Tibet was banned from practicing Celestial funerals because they were a part of the old traditions, the "Four Olds." Even though China banned the custom, Tibetans continued to follow it anyway. The Chinese people do not understand the strong Tibetan culture of Celestial burials, and there have been several clashes in recent years involving Tibetan monks fighting off Chinese crowds that would like to turn these funerals into tourist attractions.

After I returned home, I spent day after day meditating on my father, hoping to connect with his spirit. I closed my eyes in prayer, imagining that he was sitting beside me. My visualization of him was weak, but it was stronger than my other memories. The memory of the eyes lasts the longest, making imprints of images on the mind. The memory from smells, sounds, and touch do not last as long. Only the memory of pain and love can compete. With my father, there were memories of both pain and love.

As I dove deeper into a meditative state, I tapped into the micro senses of my being. I concentrated on the sound of a sound and the breath of a breath. My body and mind aligned and I was held in suspension, hanging from an invisible thread of reality.

Yet, in that moment of meditation, I saw a glimpse of the futility of my faith. Suddenly, everything that I had lived for and believed in seemed baseless. I opened my eyes and stopped meditating. I could feel my pulse increase. I felt desperately useless and weak. I didn't know what was happening, but I didn't like it. I tried to calm myself down, close my eyes, and meditate again, but I could not shake my anxiety.

I began to chant, but my voice was shaking and I started to breathe rapidly.

"What if all of this is a lie?" I asked myself. "What if the cycle of life and death is a completely made-up idea and my father's body was not carried up to the heavens by birds? What if my prayers for him are powerless because my faith and the afterlife are not real?"

I tried to stop thinking about it. It was too frightening to contemplate that my father's death was final. It was equally frightening to think that I had spent my entire life wasting away in monasteries when I could have been spending time with him.

What I was feeling was something that I needed to discuss with one of the lamas in the temple, but at the same time, it was nothing that I wanted to openly admit to. I was now a senior monk, supposedly full of wisdom and teachings from the Dalai Lama himself. My future income was now based on people coming from far and wide to ask me to pray, read, teach, and give counsel. A senior monk who no longer believed in the certainty of Buddhism was worth less than nothing in the village of Jichu.

I tried to shake these thoughts, but the more I tried, the more they continued to embed themselves in the depths of my mind.

39
THE PRECIOUS TRINITY

After I had spent a month at home mourning for my father, Tashi Lama came and asked me to return to the village monastery to be a teacher until I went back to Lhasa. It was good to see him again. The balance of our relationship had changed. I was no longer a lowly student, but I had now seen more of the world than he had, and I had studied at many prestigious monasteries.

I gladly accepted the opportunity and moved into the monastery the same day. I had a strong feeling of nostalgia when I walked into the main hall. Everything seemed familiar, and yet somehow smaller. It did not take long for me to fall back into the habits of the daily routine there.

When the locals heard that I was back for a short time to serve at the monastery, they began calling on me daily to come and pray for their children, read scriptures at their funerals, and declare blessings over their crops.

I was a reader, so my main job was to recite Tibetan writings on special occasions. I was given very good pay to read at these special events. There are hundreds of thousands of ancient Buddhist writings that most Buddhists have never seen or heard of, and none of them is available to the general public, so I read from these treasured writings for the benefit of both the monastery and the people.

It felt good to be back at the monastery, and I chalked up my doubts about Buddhism to nothing more than the product of intense sorrow and grief.

The death of my father had made me curious about the "Bardo Thodol," which, in the West, is frequently published under the title *The Tibetan Book of the Dead*. This is an ancient guide with instructions on how to journey through the stages of death until reincarnation. I started to read it for myself, as well as to read from its teachings of wisdom during the ceremonial funerals in which I was asked to recite. I had never really studied it fully, but I was more curious about it now than ever.

The *Book of the Dead* is one of the most unusual books ever written in the history of Buddhism. It gives instructions on what to do as one passes through the bardo world, or the world of transition, when the spirit transports for forty-nine days after death. According to Buddhist teachings, the number forty-nine is powerful because it is based on the square of the most sacred number, seven. There are seven worlds of Maya that rotate seven revolutions. I spent every moment I could reading this book, and there were various sections that jumped out at me:

> O nobly-born, the time hath now come for thee to seek the Path. Thy breathing is about to cease. Thy *guru* hath set thee face to face before with the Clear Light; and now thou art about to experience it in its Reality in the *Bardo* state, wherein all things are like the void and cloudless sky, and the naked, spotless intellect is like unto a transport vacuum without circumference or centre.[7]

The section about the Clear Light stood out to me because the term appeared again and again. From the text, it seemed to indicate not merely a light, but something more.

> O nobly-born, listen. Now thou art experiencing the Radiance of the Clear Light of Pure Reality.[8]

In the *Book of the Dead*, the concept of Clear Light was connected to another idea known simply as the Trinity—two entities that we could clearly expect to see in the afterlife.

---

7. W. Y. Evans-Wentz, ed. and comp., *The Tibetan Book of the Dead* (Oxford: Oxford University Press, 2000), 180, http://padmasambhavagururinpoche.com/wp-content/uploads/2017/07/padmasambhava_tibetan-book-of-the-dead_4.pdf. In this and subsequent quotes, italicized words and bracketed portions are in the original.
8. Ibid., 182.

Remember the Precious Trinity, exerting towards them fondness and faith. Whosoever thine own tutelary deity may be, recollect now; calling him by name, pray thus:

"[Alas!], wandering am I in the *Bardo*; run to my rescue; uphold me by thy grace, O precious Tutelary!"[9]

Trinity? The idea that the god I would pray to in the afterlife was three in one jumped out at me. The belief that I would call out to him to rescue me and bring me to the Clear Light was completely new for me. I read on with chills running down my spine. I felt as if I was on the precipice of discovering something new. My eyes could not read fast enough.

Calling upon the name of thine own guru, pray thus:

"[Alas!] wandering am I in the *Bardo*; rescue me! [O] let not thy grace forsake me!"[10]

Know at that time that it is the Sidpa Bardo [in which thou art]. Invoking, by name, the Compassionate One, pray earnestly, thus: "O Compassionate Lord, and my Guru, and the Precious Trinity, suffer it not that I fall into the unhappy worlds."[11]

I thought I knew that the Precious Trinity was the past, present, and future Buddha, but this text appeared to suggest something different. I kept reading.

Accordingly, pray earnestly to the Precious Trinity; that will protect thee.[12]

Call upon the Precious Trinity and take refuge [therein]. Pray unto the Great Compassionate One. Walk with thy head erect. Know thyself in the *Bardo*. Cast away all weakness and attraction towards thy sons and daughters or any relations left behind thee; they can be of no use to thee. Enter upon the White Light—[Path] of the *devas*, or upon the Yellow Light—Path of human beings;

---

9. Ibid., 277.
10. Ibid.
11. Ibid., 239.
12. Ibid., 242.

enter into the great mansions of precious metals and into the delightful gardens.[13]

The information in the *Book of the Dead* seemed to be pointing to a deity that I had not been exposed to yet. Deep down, on another level in my spirit, I felt a connection to a protecting God who would lead me and guard me in the afterlife. This text seemed to reveal that to me somehow.

I grew more curious about the triune god whom I would cry out to. The text jumped off of the pages as I read again, "Accordingly, pray earnestly to the Precious Trinity; that will protect thee."

While studying the *Book of the Dead*, I found that I was incorporating many of its ideas into the weekly debate sessions. During these times, I would often challenge two or three monks. The debate subjects were making the younger monks a bit uncomfortable and the word was getting back to Tashi Lama.

"I heard that you have been concentrating a lot on the *Book of the Dead* with your students," he said to me one day in passing at the monastery.

"I have been meditating on it more and more and—"

"And bringing it into the debates?" he quickly chimed in. "The *Book of the Dead* teaches us about the activity of the spirit world after death. It is important to concentrate on the central message and not be confused by the ancient language."

"What is confusing should be hashed out with truth," I responded.

"Truth is not found by truth seekers alone. This is the reason that we pray prior to each debate, because in order to combat the confusion of demons, we must call out to Prince Manjushri. Manjushri uses his flaming sword to fight off the demons of doubt that you cannot even see."

"Can Manjushri helps us find the Clear Light? Can his sword clear the way for us when we stand before the Trinity? Is Manjushri, with his flaming blue sword, afraid to evaluate the truth about Jesus?"

I stopped. I had blurted out that last part before even thinking about it. Tashi Lama was at a loss for words. In all the years that I had studied

---

13. Ibid., 266.

Buddhism, I had never heard anyone bring up the name of Jesus. When I had finally heard about him while in India, I had wondered why his name was never mentioned.

Tashi Lama gathered his composure. "You are never to bring up that name here in this monastery again. Do you understand?"

"Why? We are continually evaluating the thirty-three million different gods of Hinduism, so why can't we ask honest questions about Jesus in the same way we do for the thirty-three million Hindu gods?"

"Because we are not Hindus—we are Buddhists. And Jesus is not a god; he is a dangerous deceiver."

I started to reply, but instead I began to cough. The cough took me by surprise, and soon I was unable to catch my breath. I just kept coughing. I tried to stop long enough to speak again, but the more I tried, the more I coughed. I felt like I was unable to breathe.

I leaned back and braced myself against the wall. Then I put my hand over my mouth, and when I pulled it away, my palm was full of blood.

40
TUBERCULOSIS

After seeing me cough up blood, Tashi Lama had insisted that I go to Lhasa for treatment. He feared that I might have a kind of lung cancer. When I arrived, I had to wait in the lobby of the hospital for half a day before they agreed to see me.

"We are going to run some more tests to confirm, but it seems that you might have tuberculosis," the nurse said, translating for the foreign doctor into basic Chinese. "I am going to need you to stay here for a little longer so that we can run the tests."

I had no idea what *tuberculosis* meant, but I was certain that it couldn't be that bad. I felt fine. I knew I'd been intermittently battling a bit of a cough for the last year or so, but otherwise I felt fit and healthy.

The nurse walked away to attend to other matters, but the doctor stayed and continued evaluating my chart.

"How do you feel?" he asked in near-perfect Amdo Tibetan. I almost fainted with surprise. Most of the health professionals in Lhasa are Han Chinese and cannot speak the local language—nor do they try.

"Wow, you speak Tibetan?

"Yes. It is something that I have been studying on and off. I feel that I should at least know a little bit of the language if I am going to work here, right?"

I laughed. No one in China thought that way. He was truly a funny foreigner.

As he was looking over the readings from the machines in my room, I noticed that he was wearing a small, silver, t-shaped icon on his white collar. "What does that mean?" I asked, pointing to his collar.

"It is called a cross. It means that I am a follower of Jesus."

I stopped breathing. I had been desperately looking for someone who could tell me about Jesus—and now here was someone in the same room where I was who could do that.

I sat up and asked, "Are you an American? I have family members who also are followers of Jesus, and they now live in America."

He chuckled. "No, I am from a country called Sweden. It is a small nation in northern Europe."

"I have been trying to learn about Jesus, but I do not know any people who follow this faith. Can you teach me?"

"Sure, I would love to, Tenzin. Nothing would make me happier. I have to see a few other patients, but I promise that I will bring you some information about Jesus. Is that OK?"

"Yes!" I was so happy to hear that the doctor was going to teach me about Jesus that I completely forgot why I was in the hospital in the first place. After he left the room, I lay in my bed thinking of all the questions that I would ask him. I didn't know where to start. I tried to formulate the best questions that would give me the greatest understanding. The funny thing is that I don't think I would even have been very curious about Jesus at all if the monks had not forbidden me to learn about him.

Later in the evening, the doctor returned to my room and handed me two small booklets. "Here you go, Mr. Tenzin. I hope that these can help answer a few of your questions. If you would still like to know more, I can bring you additional information, but it would mainly be in the Chinese language."

"Thank you!" I said as I quickly scanned the small, precious booklets he had given me.

"I also want you to know that there are many Christians who are praying for your health."

"Can you explain to me what a Christian is?"

"*Christian* is just a name that we call those who follow Jesus. You follow the ways of Buddha, so we would call you a Buddhist. Christians who follow Jesus believe that He—the Christ—came to save the world, so we call those who follow Him Christians."

The expression on my face must have given away my deep confusion, because he reached toward me, tapped me on my shoulder, and said, "Do not worry. The booklets that I have given you will help it make sense. My language is not very good, so it is hard for me to express these things."

Although his language was broken and awkward, I was able to understand most of what he was saying. The things I did not understand had more to do with ideas than language. He was expressing an idea that I had never heard of before.

The doctor then leaned in. In a very slow, deliberate, soft voice, he said, "I am sure that you understand, but I would appreciate it if you didn't tell anyone where you got these booklets."

"I understand," I said. As a Buddhist monk, I knew that we had many teachings that were not accepted in China. We were not allowed to print or share about the teachings of the Dalai Lama because the government regarded him as an enemy of the state. If Jesus were anything like the Dalai Lama, I was certain that China would be against the sharing of his teachings as well.

As soon as the doctor exited the room, I opened up the booklets and began to read them. They had pictures on every page to help me understand.

I devoured everything in them, and I was able to finish reading them in only a short time. In fact, I read through them so fast that I felt less satisfied than if I had never read them at all. It was like sitting down for dinner after many days of not eating and having only a single grain of rice placed before you on a very big plate.

The first booklet told a story about a man named Jesus who was the Son of God. His story is recorded in a holy book that the Christians call the Bible. The Bible gives a more detailed account of how humanity rejected God and brought pain to the world through sin, and how Jesus came to earth and gave of Himself to save humanity from the damnation that sin brought.

On one page, it told how Jesus paid the price for man's sin. His grace paid the debt. This was a shocking difference between Buddha and Jesus. Buddha taught that followers had to do many things to earn their way into a better afterlife.

I was drawn in by the central theme of love. God loved the world so much that He gave His Son to die for the sin of humanity. Jesus loved people so much that He gave His own life. The followers of Jesus loved both God and people so much that they gave their lives to tell others about God's love. There just seemed to be love everywhere! It was the focal point of everything that I read.

In Buddhism, enlightenment and knowledge drive our motives, not love. Maybe you could say that we love knowledge, but you could not say that we follow Buddha because we love him or because he loved us.

I read, reread, and read again the little pamphlets the doctor had given to me. I couldn't wait to learn more.

41
THE DOCTOR'S GIFT

The following day, when the doctor came in to see how I was doing, I enthusiastically grabbed him by the arm and pulled him in closer. "How can I get a Bible?" I asked.

In the small booklets, I had read about the book called the Bible so many times that I was starting to drive myself crazy thinking about the stories that I would find inside it if I only had one.

"I do not have one in the Tibetan language, I am afraid," he said. "In fact, I do not even know if there is a complete Bible in your language."

"What do you mean? Is the Bible only allowed in certain languages?"

"No," he answered. "It just has not been completely translated into your language."

"Why?"

The doctor shrugged his shoulders. "Not sure. Maybe because there are not enough Christians in Tibet."

"What does that have to do with anything? From what I have read, it seems like the Bible is full of good stories. There are so many Christians in the world who follow this book as their religion. It would seem to me that a good student of any religion should know about Jesus and what he did."

"Oh, I totally agree with you," the doctor said. "But, unfortunately, there are many people out there who do not see it the same way. You see, ever since Jesus came to earth, people in high positions of power have wanted to destroy the history of Jesus, His teachings, His disciples, and the book that tells us about Him—the Bible. I can't explain it. All I can say is that the Bible is one of the most hated books in history."

"Does the Bible share a secret spell that can curse people?"

"No," he said calmly. "The Bible is an open book for everyone to read that blesses all people."

"If it is such a blessing, then why is it hated by so many people?"

The doctor paused, thought for a moment, and then said, "That is a good question. Sometimes evil knows that people will promptly reject evil, so it disguises itself as good and then attacks good as if it were evil. In the confusion, evil can accomplish its mission. Does that make sense?"

For me as a Buddhist, this actually did make sense.

"Oddly enough, there are a lot of people here in China who desperately want a Bible, but the government keeps them from having one."

"Why?"

"Because the truth is a powerful thing. The words of truth are sharper than any two-edged sword. Governments have been fighting to keep the Bible from getting into their societies since it was first written. The Bible has the power to move in the hearts of people in a special way."

"That doesn't scare me," I immediately said. "I have spent my entire life searching for the truth."

"Maybe," the doctor responded, "but not everyone is like you, Tenzin. Some people are deathly afraid of the truth."

"Are there writings that the Christians reject? Things that they are afraid of?"

The doctor laughed for a moment and then looked back at me and said, "No. There have been times of fear and confusion among Christian societies, but Christian societies today that are based on the Bible are actually the most free in the world. In fact, did you know that you might not have the writings of Buddhism in China if it were not for Christians?"

"What? No. You must be joking!"

"No, it is true. In fact, if you travel to the center of China, to a city called Xi'an, you will find a large stone tablet outside of a Buddhist temple. The stone tablet is over ten feet high and has writing on it in two languages—Persian and Chinese—about the first Christian to ever come to China."

I was stunned. "What did it say?"

"It told the story of a man they called Alopen who came to China to teach about Jesus during the Tang Dynasty, around the same time that Buddhism came to Tibet. The stone tablet tells how the emperor loved the teachings of the new Christians and accepted them."

I was totally blown away as the doctor talked about the story written on the stone. "Is the stone still there?"

"Yes. I have seen it. It is pretty amazing. While I was there, I also learned that during that time, there were Buddhist teachers who came to Xi'an, but they were unable to share their teachings because the court of the emperor could not read the language from India. Alopen the Christian was fluent in both Persian and Chinese, while the Buddhist monks were only fluent in Hindi and Persian. Persian was the main trade language in the East at the time. The emperor did not like the Buddhists and treated them badly, but Alopen helped them to translate the first Buddhist sutras into the Chinese language. Those sutras traveled all over China, Korea, and Japan.

"Alopen did not have a Bible translated into Hindi for the Buddhists, so he wrote some very famous sutras of his own to teach them about Jesus. Rumor is that the Buddhists from India enjoyed the writings, which are called the Jesus Sutras. One is called the *Sutra on the Origin of Origins*— about the beginning of everything. The other is called the *Sutra of Hearing the Messiah*."

"Do you have those sutras with you?"

"No, but I have something a little better." The doctor reached into his bag and pulled out a small black book. On the cover, in silver lettering, was written 圣经—the Chinese word for "Bible."

"I am sorry that I do not have a Bible in the Tibetan language, but I do have one written in Chinese. This is not an easy book to obtain. This particular one was printed by an illegal printing house inside of China. If the police find you with it, you are likely to get into trouble, so do not tell anyone where you got it from—OK?"

I nodded my head in agreement. I was happy to get my hands on the book. My Chinese was not great, but I had learned to understand a little bit over the years.

"I have to go now," he said, "but if you have any desire to learn more about what you find in that book, do not hesitate to ask."

I took the book and held it to my chest like a precious gift, running my fingers over it. I knew that it was a special thing to have a Bible in my hands. I didn't want to ever let it go.

"Would you mind if I prayed for you?"

I had no idea what he meant by that. I had spent my entire life praying. Prayer was a large part of who I was, and we prayed on behalf of the dead, but I didn't know what it meant to pray for someone who was living or what he meant by prayer as a Christian.

"I am a doctor, Tenzin, but there is only so much that I can do for your health using modern medicine alone. I believe that God loves you and wants desperately to have a relationship with you. He sees the pain of your disease, and I believe that He has the power to heal your body."

Despite my earlier optimism about my health, the nurses had told me that the chances of my surviving this disease called tuberculosis were slim. I was prepared to die. However, I nodded in agreement, and with that, the doctor walked closer to my bed, put his right hand on my right arm, and began speaking in a language I was not familiar with. Suddenly, without warning, I felt something flow through my arm. It was like a warm, soft blanket. It moved into my shoulders and chest, and then throughout my entire body.

I could not understand the doctor's words, but his prayer had something my prayers lacked—it had power. When I was a new monk, I had experienced something supernatural during Tashi Lama's prayers—but this was different.

That night, a man in a white robe came to me in my dreams. He had a glow about him that radiated in every direction. I felt warm and safe in his presence.

As he approached me, I could tell there was something wrong with his hands. In his palms were scars that had not completely healed over. I tried to look closer to see if I could catch a glimpse of his face, but I could not.

"Follow me," he said. He spoke perfect Tibetan and had a low, soothing voice like that of a loving father.

"Are you Jesus?" I asked. But again, he simply said, "Follow me."

"Are you the one to show the path to truth?"

"Follow me, Tenzin. I am the path. I am the way. I am the truth. No one comes to the path but through ne."

"OK," I answered. "I will follow you."

I woke up, sat up in bed, and looked around. I was still in the hospital, but I knew that something had changed that would make me very different.

42

FINDING JESUS

Lying in bed with nothing else to do, I thought about the dream over and over. I also scoured the pages of the Bible I had been given. I wondered if it would teach me more about the Jesus I had seen in my dream.

The Bible was a real treasure to me. I could read most of it and understand it, even though it was in the Chinese language and many of the proper names were hard for me to read because some of them had Chinese characters I had never seen before. I came across the names of cities and nations that I had never heard of, but at the back of the Bible was a small map showing where each place was. I was amazed that the places and nations were real and could be found on a map.

For me, one of the big differences between Hinduism and Buddhism is that Buddha was a real person who traveled to real places that could be visited. Following a historical Buddha rather than a mythical Vishnu was a big deal for me. How could I follow the spiritual teachings of Vishnu if there was no proof that he existed? The fact that history could prove there was a real prince who became a Buddha brought me a certain level of comfort.

It was interesting for me to learn that it was the same way with Jesus. The texts, the maps, and the names of the kings and rulers of the day seemed to indicate that Jesus, too, was a real person in history who became a spiritual leader. The more I read, the more similarities I found between Buddha and Jesus.

Like Buddha, Jesus had disciples who followed him and learned from him.

Much like Buddha, Jesus taught in parables. He used things that people could see to teach them about things they could not see.

I was surprised to read that Jesus ran the moneychangers out of the holy temple. Like Buddha, Jesus did not cater to religious ceremony. He attended to the hearts of the people.

Buddha criticized the caste system. Likewise, I came across a story about Jesus at a well talking with a woman from a different caste system. Jesus did not look at her outward features or what group of people she belonged to, but he interacted with her and accepted her.

Buddha was not liked by the Brahmins. Similarly, Jesus was hated by the teachers in His culture.

Buddha taught the Five Precepts, which teach against killing, stealing, lying, cheating, and sexual immorality. Jesus taught His disciples not to kill, steal, lie, cheat, or practice sexual immorality.

There were other parallels. Jesus's promise to return again reminded me strongly of the return of the future Buddha. Jesus, too, rejected material wealth in favor of spiritual truth. Heaven sounded much like the golden temple of the Tibetan Buddhist afterlife, with hell also sounding very much like what I had studied.

Jesus did not marry, and neither did many of His followers. This appealed to me because of the monastic lifestyle I was living.

I came across a statement that said, "But small is the gate and narrow the road that leads to life, and only a few find it."[14] I stopped and meditated on that verse. The portion about the narrow path leading to life struck me strongly. I continued reading to the next section and saw that Jesus said, "Foxes have dens and birds have nests, but the Son of Man has no place to lay his head."[15] In my life as a monk, I had felt that way many times—like I didn't have a home or a place to live. I was living only on the support of the monastery.

Again and again in the Bible, I felt as if Jesus's words were being spoken directly to me. All of his teachings were echoing deep inside of me and exposing the lack of what I had yearned for as a monk.

---

14. Matthew 7:14.
15. Matthew 8:20.

As I continued to read, I came to another section where Jesus said, "I am the way and the truth and the life."[16]

Like Buddha, Jesus emphasized truth.

Like Buddha, Jesus taught love and compassion for others and came to remove suffering from humanity.

But while there were so many similarities, I could not help seeing the differences as well.

I read the story about Jesus being killed on the cross. Jesus died to save those whom he loved. He gave his life so that everyone could come to know the truth. It was a powerful display of sacrificial love that I didn't see a parallel to in Buddha. Buddha did not give his life so that others could live.

Jesus spoke very plainly about the idea of sin against a Creator-God and the need for a Savior.

In the Bible, there was a very clear idea about the human race starting with a man and a woman, and their lineage is mapped out for several thousand years. This was much different from the Tibetan idea of a people group starting as the offspring of an evil woman and a monkey.

In Tibetan Buddhism, although there are teachings about sins and atonement, there is no place for a Savior who is capable of atoning for the sins of the world. Atonement is built on the idea of works, not grace. Faith in Jesus as the Messiah is central to the Bible, whereas Buddhism focuses on faith in self-awareness.

Over the next couple of days, while lying in bed at the hospital, I was able to do some serious introspection. I had spent the better half of my life searching for Abhidharma, or the supreme truth. I had searched for the best teachers and dedicated myself to the most holy texts. I had sat under the tutelage of His Holiness the Dalai Lama himself. Yet, in all of the prayers and meditation, I never found anything that satisfied my desire for the supreme truth.

I asked myself a question I had asked before: "Do we seek Abhidharma or do we imitate the act of seeking?" As a Buddhist monk, had I been painting only what I saw and observed, or had I been copying the paintings

16. John 14:6.

of those who had gone before me and ignoring the real landscape in front of me? Worse yet—had I been painting another reality and selling it to people as the real thing?

The more I read about Jesus, I felt like a fraud. Maybe I had not been seeking for the truth all along. Maybe I had been seeking for signs that I hoped reinforced my idea of truth.

As I thought about my desire to find the supreme truth of the Abhidharma, I came across a very special passage in the Bible: "Ask and it will be given to you; seek and you will find; knock and the door will be opened to you. For everyone who asks receives; the one who seeks finds; and to the one who knocks, the door will be opened."[17]

I closed my eyes and prayed, "Jesus, if you are there, I am knocking. I am seeking. I am asking."

43

BECOMING A FOLLOWER

"Good news, Tenzin. It looks like you are doing much better. I can't really explain it, but you no longer have any of the signs of infection in your lungs. I have looked at the X-rays and your bloodwork, and there is nothing to indicate that you should stay here. You have a clean bill of health! You are free to leave."

The doctor was clearly more excited for me to be discharged than I was to leave. For the past two weeks, I had felt that the hospital bed was my meditation cave. I hadn't had to go anywhere or do anything else. I had been able to pray and read the Bible from morning until night every day while someone brought me food and drink. I had never felt so refreshed. Reading from the Bible was like drinking from a source of fresh water. Only a few days of reading from the Bible meant more to me than several years of reading the most precious sutras.

"I thought that I was really sick. How could I be better already?"

---

17. Matthew 7:7–8.

"It truly is a miracle that you cleared up as quickly as you did, Tenzin. I wish that I could take credit for it, but I can't."

"Do you think that Jesus healed me, Doctor? You know, from when you prayed for me?"

"I think that is exactly what happened. The important thing is that you remain thankful and never forget what happened here. You promise?"

"I will never forget this," I said. I had been praying my entire life, but I had never seen any of my prayers really answered. This was an amazing feeling. I knew there was something different in the power of the name of Jesus.

"Will I see you again, Doctor?" I asked.

"I hope so, Tenzin. It has been really great to get to know you over these last couple of weeks. I pray that you will not forget our time together here."

"Could you do something for me before I leave? Could you pray to Jesus for me? I really want to know him more. Please pray that he will send me a teacher who can show me more about his ways."

The doctor smiled and took my hand. "I am going to ask you something very important, Tenzin. I want you to think very clearly about what I am saying. I know that my language is not very good. I hope that you can forgive me and try to understand what I am saying to you."

I sat quietly as he searched for the right words.

"I know that you have lived your whole life as a monk following the teachings of Buddha. I know the level of sacrifice that you have gone through and experienced, but I want to ask you if you would like to be a follower of Jesus. Would you like to ask Jesus to come and live in your heart?"

Even after reading the Bible for several days in a row, I still was not sure what Jesus coming to live in my heart meant. However, I did remember the prayer that I had prayed earlier. I was knocking. I was searching. I was asking. Maybe this was an answer to my prayer.

I nodded yes. The doctor then prayed with me and asked me to repeat some words after him, and I did so. Afterward, I gathered my things, checked out of the hospital, and headed back home to the monastery.

I felt overjoyed but, at the same time, I trembled with fear. I knew that the monastery would no longer accept me since I was a follower of Jesus. Even though I knew all of the teachings of Buddha and could teach more about the sutras than the current lamas could, I knew that they would still reject me. For them, accepting the teachings of Jesus was essentially rejecting the teachings of Buddha. There was nothing I could do or say that would convince them otherwise.

Their attachment to Buddhism was captive at its root. The bondage was so strong that reason could not touch it. It would not matter that I had found the teachings of Jesus to be adequate in my search for truth. The superstition of the monks could not be shifted. In their minds, bad things happened to those who offended their beliefs. Fears of suffering, starvation, destruction, and death—these were just a few of the fears that kept us imprisoned. We were afraid that if we offended the spirits, these things could happen to us. It was an invisible prison.

Because of their fear, the monks did not even recognize the pain of the bondage they lived in. They only believed that things would get worse if they did not do as they were told.

My eyes were more open now than they had ever been—and it was a dangerous thing.

In Tibet, we live in poverty. We constantly live with disease and death all around us. We have a lack of food, clean water, education, and jobs. Ironically, Tibetans fear poverty even though they wade through it their entire lives and do not know anything else. They fear a lack of food even though they are constantly starving. They fear death even though they face it every day.

Tibetans fear the wrath of the demons and attempt to appease them, knowing that the demons themselves are the only things that they really need protection from. The religion that they serve does not serve them. The gods that they fear do nothing for the devout. The Tibetans have labored in vain since the beginning of Buddhism....

I needed to tell the others. I needed to set them free from the bondage that had held us all for so long.

As I traveled home, I could feel a battle raging inside of me. It was as if demons were perched on each of my shoulders, trying to discourage me. But although they whispered in my ear, I had been touched in a special way. I had seen the miraculous hand of Jesus work in my own life and could not be convinced otherwise.

The fear that had gripped me started to thaw like ice in the warm spring air. At first, it began to dissolve slowly, but then it began to drip faster and faster. Once it was removed, I felt that I was free and that fear could never be reapplied in my life in the same way again. Fear would never have the same effect as it had before it lost its power.

In a way, I was going through another Rite of Chod. I was dying to myself. I was putting to death the only man that I had ever known and giving life to a new force inside of me. That new force was not full of fear but love. That love was Jesus Christ. "I have been crucified with Christ and I no longer live, but Christ lives in me. The life I now live in the body, I live by faith in the Son of God, who loved me and gave himself for me."[18]

When I arrived at the monastery, I called for a special counsel of the monks. I knew that I had to share the good news of what I had discovered with every teacher at the monastery. I requested a special debate with Tashi Lama.

I knew that once I took this step, there would be no looking back. I also knew that once I explained the revelation of Truth that I had discovered, I might not make it out of the monastery alive. However, in my opinion, my life was no longer my own. I had been spared in the hospital. I had been given a chance to continue living for a reason. Every minute that I lived past my time at the hospital was a moment of debt and gratitude to Jesus. "For to me, to live is Christ and to die is gain."[19]

---

18. Galatians 2:20.
19. Philippians 1:21.

44
CHALLENGING THE SYSTEM

The murmurs from the gathering monks sounded like the buzz of a mosquito growing closer and closer to the ear. The monastery finally had something interesting happening—an open debate.

The debate challenge was not officially announced. It was just supposed to be my effort to introduce what I had found and to see if it could hold up under the scrutiny of a common Tibetan monastery debate. No one knew what I was going to talk about, but they knew that it had to be huge because I had openly challenged the lama. There were rumors swirling around that I wanted to take over the monastery.

What I really wanted was to discuss what I had learned about Jesus. I was not going to promote Jesus at the debate without admitting that I might be wrong. I was willing to concede that I had been tricked. I was willing to admit that maybe I had been fooled into believing something that would not lead me to the path of enlightenment. I only hoped that Tashi Lama maintained the same amount of integrity in the search for truth.

The courtyard was unusually full. Tashi Lama marched out from the front of the monastery followed by a train of disciples and supporters. Among those walking with him was my older brother, Duuka. I stood in the courtyard and watched. Tashi Lama was surrounded by the community leaders and a few visiting lamas. He had the support of all of the villagers on his side. I stood alone. I would be lying if I said that I was not intimidated.

Sweat beaded up on my forehead. My hands fidgeted. Without prayer beads to count, I did not know what else to do to keep my fingers occupied. I felt like I was standing there naked. Every fiber of my being was screaming at me to run for the hills. I could easily go into hiding in another monastery in Tibet. I could find a small monastery in Qinghai or Sichuan

Province to eke out the rest of my life with little or no humiliation. I didn't need to go through with this.

At that moment, I wished I had tuberculosis again. I wanted to go back to the safety of my hospital bed. However, at the same time, I felt an unexplainable strength from within that kept my feet planted. It was a strength that spoke to me with a still, small voice and told me that I could do this. My legs were shaking and my hands were quivering, but my heart was still and my mind was clear.

I thought of the story I had read about Jesus in the garden before His crucifixion. He had asked for the "cup" of persecution to pass by Him if it were possible, but He prayed, "Yet not my will, but yours be done."[20] I did not know exactly what that meant, but I whispered to the heavens, "Not my will, but Yours be done."

The crowd had grown so large that people had to squeeze against each other to allow Tashi Lama to walk through. A red pillow had already been placed on the ground for him to sit on. He walked up to me, bowed, turned, looked up, and began to chant the mantra to the Buddha of Wisdom. After chanting the mantra, he lowered himself onto the pillow. The battle lines had been drawn, and now everyone waited for the first shot to be fired.

I stood silent, not knowing what to say. There was a long, uncomfortable silence.

After about a minute of awkwardness, Tashi Lama smirked and began to look around, bobbing his head at his friends. They responded to him with knowing laughter.

"Have you nothing to say?" Tashi Lama asked.

I did have something to say. I had a lot to say, but I didn't know how to start or even if I should start. I knew that I had to say something, but I was not able to say anything. I just stood there in silence.

"I remember when you first came to this monastery when you were just a young boy. You were not the best student. You were never good at memorizing scripture or learning the essentials of prayer, but I tried to be patient with you and give you a chance to better yourself. It is clear that

20. Luke 22:42.

after all these years and all of the experiences that you have had, they have not brought you closer to the path. They say that wisdom comes with age, but in your case, age has come alone."

The crowd laughed. Tashi Lama lifted up his hands, signaling for someone to help him up.

"Wait!" I said with a slight, high-pitched crack in my voice. "Do you desire to leave before we even start?" I didn't say it, but it was as if I was telling him to sit back down. The crowd recognized it as a challenge.

"Oh, so the mute speaks," Tashi Lama said in a condescending voice.

"Om mani padme hummmmm." I drew out the last syllable and chanted again. "Om mani padme hummm."

The crowd was shocked. No one ever chants in the middle of a debate. It was appropriate to chant before and after a debate, but never during it. It was clear that I was not following the rules.

"Through mantra, we no longer cling to the reality of life but instead attempt to awaken the spirits to aid us," I said as I banged my hands together and stomped my right foot.

Tashi Lama did not verbally answer. Instead, he just nodded his head.

"In this way, experience is essentially empty when compared to the experience of the spirits. The mantra beckons the aid of the spirits and asks them to guide us with what they know, even if it contradicts our experience. Enlightenment and awareness through experience is inferior to the insight of the spiritual world, for they can see and have seen what we cannot see. Through the guiding of the spirits, we can be saved from suffering if we are sensitive to what they are telling us. Obtaining holy dharma is said to be contained in these six syllables that I have just chanted."

Tashi Lama did not respond.

I continued, "The technical translation of this mantra is secondary to the fact that it is this mantra that our people believe represents the purification of the six realms of existence. The six realms of existence, or the samsara, are the beginning-less cycle of birth and rebirth in one of these six realms of three heavens and three hells. Samsara is the mundane existence of being born, living, suffering, dying, and being born again. The entire cycle is riddled with suffering, anguish, and pain. The Buddha set out on a quest that we now follow to find the way to end this suffering. These are the foundational principles of Buddhism."

I wasn't clapping or allowing Tashi Lama to agree or disagree. The entire flow of my argument was unorthodox, but the argument itself was rudimentary. I knew that their patience toward me had already been worn thin because I had presented an open challenge to Tashi Lama, so I continued to push through with brevity. I could feel the audience hanging on my every word, ready to cheer for Tashi Lama when he "put me in my place."

"This world that we exist in is the suffering-laden cycle of life, death, and rebirth without beginning or end. We wander from one life to another with no particular direction or purpose. Our life is characterized by dukkha—the unsatisfactory pain of a pointless life. Our only hope is to escape it all by working hard to obtain enough points to earn karma, which will propel us into nirvana—a state where suffering and existence cease." At this, I stomped my feet and clapped my hands together.

My words were simple enough that every single person listening could follow along. Everything that I stated about Buddhism would have been thoroughly known by even the most uneducated person in the crowd.

"Is this what you have called me out here to discuss in front of all these people, Tenzin? Do you need me to teach you the elementary subject of the Four Noble Truths?" Tashi Lama asked.

The people laughed.

"No, I have called you out here to ask, 'How do you know that the life-cycle is pointless? What if there is a purpose to suffering?'"

The crowd went silent. During a debate, monks are supposed to make statements, not ask questions.

"We spend our entire life suffering, and Buddha was supposed to illuminate the path that leads to the elimination of suffering, but who has escaped suffering by following the path? I would argue that we add to it. When we follow the path illuminated by the Buddha, we add to our own dukkha."

The crowd gasped.

"The entire merit-based system is exhausting! We are told to do so many things that lead to more suffering, and the additional suffering helps to accumulate merits that will contribute to the karma of the next life. We are commanded to stand, kneel, lay prostrate, spin wheels, chant, meditate, give offerings, give money, not eat, not marry, leave our family—the merit-earning never ends. Can suffering more lead to less suffering later on? After all of these years, I have to ask if our merit is enough to end suffering. What if we are not able to earn enough merit to end dukkha and experience nirvana? What if someone greater than we are is needed to end the suffering once and for all?"

"Enough!" Tashi Lama said. "You are bringing judgment on us all by questioning the Buddha and offending the gods."

"More judgment? You mean more than we already have? Look around at the suffering of our people. We are sick with no cure. We are hungry with no food. We are poor with no jobs. We are thirsty with no clean water. What have our merits earned us in heaven or on earth? Tashi Lama, I have seen you pray for hours and days and weeks. What have your prayers earned you? I have seen the people here spin prayer wheels until their arms could no longer be held up, and what mercy did they get?"

"Stop him!" Tashi Lama yelled out.

"Wait!" I held up my hand to delay the monks who were prepared to grab me. "Tashi Lama, what if I told you that there was a way to obtain merits that you did not earn?" Suddenly, the monks who were prepared to grab me waited to hear more.

45
"KILL HIM!"

"What if all of the merits that you have been trying to earn have already been earned and are now offered to you—not by works, but by grace?"

There was a pause from Tashi Lama.

"Om mani padme hummmmm," I chanted again and held out my hands in the chanting pose meant to channel the energy.

"When we chant mantras, what are we doing? We are beckoning the aid of the spirit world to give us insight about something we do not understand—right? What if we need help from the spirit world not just to help with understanding, but to help with merit?"

I felt that what I was saying was starting to make sense to everyone around me. I could tell that they were waiting for me to explain more to them.

"What if I told you that I prayed to a God who said that He could guide me through the spirit world and I did not have to earn merits to hear from Him because He gave it all to me by grace. I could not earn it on my own."

The crowd was breathlessly silent. Not even prayer beads could be heard rolling through the rough knuckles of aged monks.

"When I was lying in bed in the hospital, I was told about a God who gave His life for me so that I would not have to suffer dukkha any longer. He did not do it because I had earned enough merits. He did it because He loved me. His love leads to the path that ends suffering, and His name is Jesus."

"Grab him now!" Tashi Lama shouted.

"Kill him!" the crowd screamed. "He is a Christian! Kill him!"

Suddenly, I was shoved to the ground and surrounded by several monks. My face was pushed into the dirt and I could feel the sharp jabs of feet kicking me in the ribs.

I felt my hair being pulled. I hadn't shaved my head for a while and there was some growth on top, and the monks' hands were plucking at the stubble, but it wasn't giving them enough of a grip. Then someone latched their hands around my head and laced their fingers at the bottom of my chin and started to drag me backward across the dirt.

I was choking and so I tried to propel myself with my feet in the direction that my head was being pulled, but there were too many people around.

That is all I remember.

The next thing I knew, I was sitting on a dirt floor in the center of the temple. I could taste the blood in my mouth. I swallowed it.

I saw a fist coming down toward my face and tried to block it with my hands, but it was too late. I could feel my teeth coming loose and hoped that none of them had been knocked out. If I could only have seen the person hitting me, it might have been easier to dodge the punches, but it was hard to see. The dim light coming from the bare lightbulb hanging from the ceiling was clouded by the mist of dry dust swirling around the room.

The monks from my village surrounded me in murderous rage. They seethed with anger and feelings of betrayal and paced around me like predators moving in for the kill. They did not just want to kill me—they wanted to slowly filet me with all of their accusations and force me to bathe in the shame of my choice before executing me. I was not sure that I wanted to resist them. My will to live was growing weaker by the second.

There were too many people punching me at the same time. Even if I could have seen enough to dodge one punch, it would have been impossible to dodge the second or third. I clinched my eyes closed. Maybe if I refused to acknowledge my attackers, they would tire out and leave me alone.

The monks who were beating me taught that pain is derived from desire. It might also be true that pain creates desire, because I had a strong desire for them to stop punching and kicking me! Ironically, it was my pain and hopelessness from following the ways of Buddha that had birthed the *desire* to know Truth and that *desire* had led me to this painful beating. So maybe the Buddhists were right—desire does lead to pain—but they only teach one part of the formula.

"You are a disgrace to the Tibetan people," one of the senior monks yelled before he delivered another pounding blow with a hammer fist to the top of my head. The pain shot from my head and traveled all the way down my spine. I convulsed with agony. Immediately, I went into a protective fetal position to cover up as much of my body as possible.

I was reminded of the beatings I had received in the early days when I would recite a verse wrong. The senior monk would yell at me and hammer me on the head with his fist. Sometimes, he would use a wooden rod to crack me across the skull. I was younger then, and the blow to the head was not delivered with as much anger as now, but the pain was comparable.

Standing all around me were the senior and junior monks of the monastery where I had spent much of my life. This temple had been my home since I was a boy, but now it was my prison. The monks surrounding me were supposed to be as close to me as my family, but tonight they were my worst enemies. They were doing whatever they thought would please Tashi Lama.

My own brother had helped the monks capture me. He was infuriated more than anyone when he heard that I had chosen to follow after the truth of Jesus Christ.

Even in my pain, there were so many things that did not make sense to me. I thought that arguments were supposed to be won or lost in debate sessions. I didn't even get to see if I had won or lost the debate with Tashi Lama.

I had dedicated my life to exactly the same search for enlightenment that all of my accusers had, and now I was going to be killed because I had not arrived at the same conclusion. My dedication had been as devoted as theirs. My sacrifices had been as great as theirs. But because I had arrived at a different determination, I would pay for it with my life.

I thought that the entire purpose of learning the ways of Buddha was to find truth and the path that would end suffering. All the years that I had spent praying, fasting, reading scriptures, leading a life of sacrifice, and not seeing my family were supposed to have led to enlightenment. My life of self-denial had been meant to lead up to an ultimate truth, but it turns out that the Truth I had discovered was an unacceptable one. The truth that the monks wanted me to accept had already been arranged. It was not discoverable; it was predetermined. They did not offer freedom; they were the wardens of a spiritual prison.

Freedom of thought to reach spiritual enlightenment had always been an illusion. Tashi Lama was not there to illuminate paths; he was there to guard the order, and he would stop at nothing to ensure its longevity. There is nothing he wouldn't have done and no one he wouldn't have killed to ensure that Buddhism prevailed even when it had been proven to fail.

I had been convinced that the entire foundation of Buddha's teachings would crumble and fall if it were forced to compare itself to the teachings of Jesus. I was convinced about the authority of Jesus Christ and the truth of His teachings, and not even the threat of death could change my mind.

I held strong to my convictions.

As I was being beaten and kicked, I was able to peek under my arm for a moment, and I saw my brother Duuka. He had a look of despair on his face. He was participating in the beating, but his face showed that he was doing so reluctantly.

I knew that he *needed* to beat me. If he did not beat me, they would surely beat him. I wished there was a way that I could communicate with him that I understood. I longed to release him of any guilt or pain that he might suffer, either now or later, for helping the mob capture and beat me.

I felt sorry for Duuka. He was as much a victim as I was at that moment. But his prison was worse than mine. I knew that I was suffering for Truth. I did not fear what human beings could do to me. Although I did not want to endure pain or suffering, that feeling did not hold me captive enough to abandon Truth in an attempt to avoid it.

Tashi Lama wanted to hear me scream for mercy. He wanted to hear me beg for my life and deny the teachings of Jesus, but unlike him, I had hope in death. Death was no longer a part of a meaningless cycle or reincarnation. Death had meaning because life in Jesus had meaning. The mob of monks did not intimidate me because I knew that death was not the end. It was only the beginning.

I knew that I would have to suffer. Ironically, the Christian path might not lead to less suffering than the Buddhist path, but only one path eventually leads to reward. The path of Buddha involves suffering, but it only leads to more suffering. What a tragedy for those who suffer without gain.

Both Jesus and Buddha suffered, but only One suffered for a purpose and only One suffered so that others would not have to.

I recalled a passage in the Bible from the book of Romans that said:

We were therefore buried with him through baptism into death
in order that, just as Christ was raised from the dead through

the glory of the Father, we too may live a new life. For if we have been united with him in a death like his, we will certainly also be united with him in a resurrection like his. For we know that our old self was crucified with him so that the body ruled by sin might be done away with, that we should no longer be slaves to sin—because anyone who has died has been set free from sin. Now if we died with Christ, we believe that we will also live with him. For we know that since Christ was raised from the dead, he cannot die again; death no longer has mastery over him. The death he died, he died to sin once for all; but the life he lives, he lives to God.[21]

I knew that I must die to myself so that I could live in Christ. And if I could live in Christ, then, although they would kill my body, I would live again with Him also.

In that moment, I no longer feared death.

Although I was on the floor being kicked and punched by everyone in the room, I was not their prisoner. I was being beaten as a free man. I had more hope in that moment than all of the other men there. I was no longer a prisoner of Buddha. They were. I was being beaten for leaving Buddha, and they were beating me because they were too afraid to.

46
ESCAPE

"Follow Me," I heard Him say again. I still could not see His face, but I knew who He was. His white, flowing robe beamed with glorious light. I felt so safe in His presence.

"I want to, Jesus. Please help me. They are killing me."

"Follow Me, My child," He repeated.

I woke up on the cold, dusty ground with a hand clamped tightly over my mouth. I found it hard to breathe, and I instinctively struggled to get air, but the hand pushed tighter against my mouth.

21. Romans 6:4–10.

"Shhhhhh," came the hushed sound from a face in the dark that I was trying to make out. "Quiet. They will hear you."

It was Duuka.

He slowly removed his hand from my mouth and brought his index finger to his lips, cautioning me to remain quiet. Then he put his arms under mine and lifted me to help me stand.

"Uffff." A sharp pain in my side pressed a sound out of my mouth that I hadn't meant to make. Duuka instantly covered my mouth again. Then, in a quick motion, he pulled part of a ripped rope, which had been resting on my shoulder, and put it in my mouth. "Bite on this if you feel pain," he whispered.

I nodded. Putting my arm around his shoulder, I limped beside him up to the door. Slowly, he unlatched the handle and opened the door just enough to look through a narrow crack. After seeing that the hallway was clear, he opened the door wide enough for us to walk through it.

We both crouched down and walked close to the wall, trying to avoid detection. As we got closer to the main entrance, I could hear a faint sound in the background over the night crickets. Even though it was muffled, it sounded like yelling.

When we got to the entrance, Duuka propped me up against the wall for a moment as he slowly cracked open the door and peeked through. Confirming that it looked clear, he opened the door a little bit more, reached back, grabbed my arm, and threw it over his shoulder. Together, we stepped over the wooden threshold and into the night air.

I could see the bright light of a fire in the distance, and I immediately recognized the location of the blaze as my mother's house.

"What's happening?"

"They are burning our mother's house."

"What? Why? She had nothing to do with this."

"None of us had anything to do with this. Mother told them that she was completely against your ideas of teaching about Jesus. They demanded that she deny Jesus publicly, which she did without delay. But it was not enough to satisfy their rage."

"Wait!" I said, stopping to grab my side. "We have to go back. We can't let them harm our mother."

"Do not worry. She is no longer there. Our brother helped her to escape to his wife's village. We have to leave now or they will kill us both."

"Why would they kill you?" I asked him. "You helped them...." I was not able to finish the sentence.

"I am sorry," he said with a cringe as we continued to move forward. "I thought that they were just going to rough you up. I had no idea they wanted to kill you. I also had nothing to do with their going after our mother."

"Why didn't they kill me?" I asked.

"They planned to beat you to death and then burn your body. You really got Tashi Lama upset. He wants your head on a platter."

"For what?"

"For someone who is escaping death, you sure have a lot of questions. Just be glad that I was able to get you out of there."

"Yeah, but seriously, what was so bad that I deserved death and my mother deserved to lose her home?"

"You corrupted the dharma, Tenzin. You soiled the well. Being of unsound conduct, virtue, mind, and discernment, you gave full permission to others to question the path. Those new monks who will be the leaders of tomorrow, and who are still undeveloped in mind and spirit, have now been corrupted. From the teachings of corrupt dharma come corrupt disciples. A poisoned well contaminates the entire spring for generations."

"But don't we challenge each other every day in debates? Are those debates real or are they nothing more than planned arguments? Are our teachings so weak that they can't withstand the challenge of outside thoughts?" I was limping along the trail that led to the mountains as fast as I could, and I was trying to squeeze out my words without running out of breath.

"But *Jesus*, Tenzin? Of all the names to mention, you had to mention Jesus? Tashi Lama would have listened to you if it had been any other name. You could have mentioned Bhrama, Vishnu, or even the evil god of

Kali. You could have mentioned your ancestors or one of the Bön gods or goddesses. Even Allah, the god of the Muslims, would have been allowed, but not Jesus."

I stopped for a moment and said, "Yes, but haven't you ever wondered why that is? Why is Jesus the only name that we cannot mention?"

"Because Jesus is the evil Mara. He has the power to confuse those trying to find the path."

"But…" I interjected.

My brother turned to face me in the starlight and put his finger up to my nose. "Listen, I am here risking my life to save your butt. I might not even make this out alive. I do not need to be subjected to your babbling. I heard enough of it already in the debates. You are my brother and that is why I am here. If you keep talking, I might leave you out here for the wolves to eat. Now shut your mouth and keep going."

I had more to say, but I understood. Duuka did not want to make waves. He didn't take a hard stand for right and wrong. He just wanted things to work out in the most painless way possible.

After we had walked for a couple of hours, we came to a little house on the edge of a nearby village. There was a small candle flickering in the back window.

"That house right there. Go up to the window with the candle and rap on the glass. They will open the door to you. In two days, someone will come and drive you to the city of Chengdu. No one there will care who you are or where you come from. It is a large city with a diverse population."

"Thank you, Duuka. I will never forget this."

"And one more thing, Tenzin," he said just before I headed for the house.

"What is that?"

"For as long as you live, you can never return to the village."

I heard myself gulp as I swallowed back my tears.

"I am serious. They threw stones at our mother, burned her house down, and want our entire family dead. This is not likely to go away soon, Tenzin. You are not welcome back."

And with that, Duuka turned and left.

EPILOGUE: WHERE THE LOTUS FLOWER GROWS

"How do you feel, Amrita?" I asked when I saw her come out into the hallway from her room.

"So great!" she said with a big smile on her face. It was wonderful to see her smiling again. Her full face was evidence that she had been gaining weight since she came to live at our House of Hope in Chengdu only a couple of months earlier.

"Praise the Lord," I exclaimed.

"Yes! Praise the Lord."

"Now remember to share your testimony with everyone in your village when they ask how you were healed of cancer," my wife, Mapu, said as she went to the kitchen. "You tell them that you were healed by the power of Jesus. By no other name is there such a power to heal."

"Amen," Amrita said.

I grabbed a handful of tracks and teaching materials from my office and gave them to her. "Please take these with you as well."

"Oh, thank you, Tenzin. You and your family have been such a blessing to me. I do not know how I will ever repay you."

"We are all saved by grace," I said.

"Amen," said a voice from one of the other bedrooms.

The House of Hope is a home my wife and I started in 2012 beside the hospital in Chendu where many Tibetans go when they are sick. We started the house to serve those who have nowhere to stay when they are in the city seeking medical treatment. Such treatment in China is often too expensive for Tibetans to afford. Unlike my experience with the missionary doctor, whom I later learned had helped pay for my expenses, most Tibetans go broke and find themselves on the street when they are in need of medical care.

Our ministry assists Tibetans during their time of need. We give them a free place to live, serve them, and share with them about the hope of Jesus Christ. It has been one of the most amazing ways to share about Jesus.

I met Mapu in Chengdu while talking with Tibetans about the message of Jesus. She became one of my first converts, and she and I fell in love. Of all the things that I love most about being a Christian, being married to Mapu is among those at the top. I never thought that I would find a woman to spend the rest of my life with. From a young age, I thought I was doomed to a life of monastic living, but I am so thankful that the Lord chose someone for me to love and to love me back. Together, we have two boys whom we absolutely adore and whom I hope will grow up to serve the Lord.

Mapu and I run a small underground house church inside our ministry home. Several Tibetan believers from around the city join us every Sunday. We are among only thirty Christians living in the midst of eight million Buddhists in our region. Because of persecution from the Chinese government, we have to be careful not to allow our fellowship to grow too big. For the most part, the government does not spend too much time watching our work. We are still pretty small and are not significant enough to draw their attention. They are more worried about the Tibetan Buddhist monk activists who want to thwart their power than they are about us.

However, because we are connected to several underground house church believers and have received discipleship training from wanted Christian felons, the local police still keep an eye on us. For the most part, the police do not give us too hard of a time because, in the end, whether it is legal or illegal, my wife and I provide a much-needed, free public service. According to the Communist government, all citizens of China should receive free access to healthcare, but it is a promise they cannot keep. Healthcare in China is expensive, and it is even more expensive for Tibetans. Tibetans do not have doctors or health clinics in their villages. They are the forgotten people of China.

Hospitals in China are located in the places that can afford to have them—places where Han Chinese live. So when Tibetans are desperate for medical care, they have no choice but to go to the cities. It is pretty hopeless, really. The Tibetans cannot speak the language of the healthcare providers and they cannot afford the bills. The Chinese medical staff know this and therefore often turn them away.

Over the years, though, I have been able to play the part of a liaison. I serve as a translator, take the patients to the proper places they need to go to for care, assist in filling out their paperwork, help get their medications, and provide a free place for them to live while they are treated. Christians from around China have come alongside our family to help to provide the funding needed to keep the operation going.

We have seen countless families changed. Many people have accepted Christ and been baptized, and there have been numerous testimonies about God moving in miraculous ways—such as in the life of Amrita.

As I helped Amrita pack her belongings, I heard the phone ring.

"I got it!" my wife yelled. Then she called out, "Honey…" indicating that the phone call was for me.

"Yes, who is it?" I asked.

"It is your brother Duuka. He is wondering when you are coming to your village again."

In the last couple of years, I have been working with a group of Chinese who have a vision called "Back to Jerusalem." It is a vision among the underground house church in China to complete the Great Commission. We have been translating videos and Bible-teaching materials into the Tibetan language. For centuries, the enemy, Satan, has kept the Bible out of the hands of the Tibetan people, but today we are working to translate God's Word so that we can distribute it wherever the Tibetan language is spoken. Word has gotten around that a former Buddhist monk is a Christian evangelist and is helping the poor get access to healthcare and Jesus's teachings.

My brother Duuka and many of the other monks at the monastery in my hometown contracted a bacterial infection of the stomach that became endemic among Tibetans. Monasteries were hit the hardest because of their lack of hygiene when gathering and consuming water.

Many monks and lamas had been dying from this bacterial infection. A number of the monks who were able to escape to India were studied for the disease and given the proper medication to treat it, but those in the rural areas of Tibet were not as fortunate. Even my mother was infected with the disease and passed away because of it.

When I heard about the problem, I traveled back to my village and met with the leadership, offering to help. My wife had begged me not to go. She was afraid for my life and thought that the monks and villagers would kill me if they found out that I had returned to the village. I knew that most of them wanted to kill me because they felt I had betrayed them. However, I could not sleep knowing that God had allowed us to have the means to save them. I had to do something with what God had placed in my hands. I knew that because Jesus loved them, then I needed to love them as well—even if they hated me. I wanted to be there to serve them and show them the love of Jesus, and I would do so—even if they killed me. Jesus taught His disciples to love their enemies: "You have heard that it was said, 'Love your neighbor and hate your enemy.' But I tell you, love your enemies and pray for those who persecute you, that you may be children of your Father in heaven."[22]

When I met with the village leadership and shared with them my idea to bring doctors and medicine to the village with a mobile clinic, there was a reluctant acceptance of my presence. They resented me, but they also knew that they would see more people die if they did not allow me to act quickly to help. In 2017, we were able to bring a mobile unit to the village and provide medical attention for more than a thousand people—not just for those in my village but also for people in the surrounding villages.

I was sitting at this mobile clinic when Tashi Lama walked in. He was waiting in line behind ten other people. There was so much rushing around by the medical workers that they did not notice he was any different from the other patients.

I immediately jumped up and grabbed a chair for him. "Please, sit here," I said. I bowed low to honor him. His eyes grew as big as plates when he saw me. I stayed bowed before him and honored him as the great teacher.

I was not wearing my crimson robes any longer. I had not worn them since the day I escaped from the monastery. I had grown my hair out,

22. Matthew 5:43–45.

although it was still rather short. I had also gained a little weight since the last time we had seen each other (I guess that is what good food from a dear wife will do for a man).

"Doctor," I shouted across the mobile unit, "please attend to this honorable patient here. He is next. Give him whatever he needs right away." Tashi Lama looked up at me as if to start to say something, but I kept moving so as to not stand on ceremony.

Later the next day, I met with the local leaders again, and all the monks from the monastery, including Tashi Lama, attended the meeting. It was so good to see my brother Duuka for the first time since he had helped me escape. The leaders had asked me to give a presentation of something else I was proposing to the village. So, that evening, in front of the village leaders, the monks, and Tashi Lama, I unveiled a plan to build the very first health clinic in Jichu Township. The clinic would be staffed by four, full-time medical workers and would provide immunizations, inoculations, and prenatal and postnatal care. It would be the front line of defense against bacterial and viral infections common among Tibetans.

The monastery leaders did not warmly embrace my plan, but they did not reject it either. I knew that dealing with me was not going to be easy for them. I respected them and wanted them to know that I just desired to help. I wanted them to know that I loved them no matter what they thought of me. Even if they tried to kill me again, I would not stop loving them.

When I walked out of that meeting, I felt the joy of the Lord fill my heart. During the entire drive home, I praised and worshipped Him for all of His endless mercies.

As I pulled into the parking lot of our building, I could see my oldest son playing with the other kids. "Welcome home, Daddy!" he yelled as he ran over to me and jumped into my arms.

"Wow! You are getting so big. I can barely carry you."

"Where did you go?" he immediately inquired.

"I took a drive to my village."

"Why did you go there? Mommy said that those mean people want to kill you."

"Oh, they are not so mean. They just do not know any better. They are like a lotus flower."

"What do you mean?"

"Well, did you know that the Tibetan people consider the lotus flower to be one of the most beautiful flowers of all? You see it painted everywhere Tibetans live. The lotus flower is a rose-and-white-colored blossom that can be found all over the world. However, it does not grow without extreme opposition from its own environment. In fact, every lotus flower comes from the mud.

"Unlike all the other flowers, its seed is found in the mud where no other life is birthed. The seed is completely surrounded by muck, insects, and murky water. These rough conditions choke out almost all forms of plant life—but not the lotus flower. The lotus struggles in these conditions but still somehow finds the strength and nutrients to grow. At the bottom of the murky water, things are confusing, opaque, and dark, but a true lotus flower will keep pushing to seek the clarity of daylight above the tepid waters. It will use all of its strength and passion to overcome the obstacles.

"For anyone watching the process, the lotus flower, while in the muddy waters, is nothing more than a plain, ugly stem. But once it pierces through the surface and finds the sunlight shining down, it blooms and becomes what it is truly meant to be—not one of the mud weeds living among the insects, but, instead, a gorgeous flower that brings beauty to that mucky swamp.

"You see, son, many of the people who do not like me are merely lotus flowers still caught in the mud. They only seem angry because they are surrounded by anger, but once they reach the clarity given by the Son and break past the confusion of their current environment, they will bloom into the most beautiful flowers you have ever seen."

Tenzin Lahkpa continues to be a wholehearted follower of Jesus Christ, serving the Tibetan people in innovative ways that meet their spiritual and physical needs and demonstrate the love of God.

About the Authors

TENZIN LAHKPA (a pseudonym) is a former Tibetan Buddhist monk who is now the leader of a Christian house church in China and assists Tibetans in receiving much-needed healthcare services. He also works with Back to Jerusalem, Inc., to translate Bible-teaching materials into the Tibetan language.

EUGENE BACH (a pseudonym) leads the Chinese mission movement Back to Jerusalem, Inc., which provides support to Chinese missionaries in Africa, Asia, and the Middle East. He has written or coauthored several books about the underground church in China, North Korea, and Iran. His previous books with Whitaker House include *The Underground Church* (with Brother Zhu), *I Stand with Christ* (with Zhang Rongliang), *Smuggling Light* (with Esther Chang), *Kidnapped by a Cult* (with Shen Xiaoming), and *ISIS: Heart of Terror.*

Welcome to Our House!

We Have a Special Gift for You

It is our privilege and pleasure to share in your love of Christian books. We are committed to bringing you authors and books that feed, challenge, and enrich your faith.

To show our appreciation, we invite you to sign up to receive a specially selected **Reader Appreciation Gift**, with our compliments. Just go to the Web address at the bottom of this page.

God bless you as you seek a deeper walk with Him!

┌─────────────────────────────────────┐
  WE HAVE A GIFT FOR YOU. VISIT:
└─────────────────────────────────────┘

whpub.me/nonfictionthx

WHITAKER
HOUSE